Media Sense

Media Sense:

The Folklore-Popular Culture Continuum

Peter Narváez and Martin Laba, editors

Bowling Green State University Popular Press
Bowling Green, Ohio 43403

Acknowledgements

Joseph R. Smallwood, "The Barrelman": The Broadcaster as Folklorist, reprinted with permission. This article was originally published in *Canadian Folklore canadien*, 5:1-2 (1983), 60-78.

Library of Congress Catalogue Card No.: 86-70527

ISBN: 0-87972-343-2 Clothbound
     0-87972-344-0 Paperback

CONTENTS

Introduction:
The Folklore-Popular Culture Continuum

The Editors

THIS VOLUME OF ESSAYS arises out of a growing concern with establishing a folkloristic perspective on contemporary popular culture.[1] As the expression is used here, popular culture refers, in a restrictive interpretation, to cultural events which are transmitted by technological media and communicated in mass societal contexts.[2] Accordingly, the performance contexts of popular culture are usually characterized by significant spatial and social distances between performers and audiences. In contrast to popular culture, folklore performance is artistic performance which is transmitted and communicated by the sensory media of living, small group encounters.[3] The spatial and social distances between performers and audiences in folklore events is slight or non-existent and there tends to be a high degree of performer-audience interaction. These conceptions of folklore and popular culture focus upon media of transmission and group size rather than on socio-economic class or matters of content. As artistic forms of communication, both folklore and popular culture demand creative enactment within a wide variety of conventionalized systems that engender and disseminate their own aesthetics and traditions. Thus, it is the procedures and contexts of stylized human behaviors which may be identified by the analyst of cultural communication in order to discern the folkloric and popular qualities of a given performance and thereby establish *media sense*.

In keeping with Russel Nye's view "to consider all levels of artistic accomplishment as related rather than disparate," artistic communication within small groups (folklore) and mass societies (popular culture) may be understood as polar types spanned by a complex continuum of different sized groups in which communications are transmitted via various configurations of sensory and technological media.[4]

Although the contents of the folklore-popular culture continuum exhibit conservative *and* dynamic qualities, the proclivities or biases of the media of artistic communications have sometimes led to oversimplified associations of folklore with conservativism, and popular culture with dynamism. What Harold A. Innis called the "time bias" of sensory media ("oral tradition") has inclined much small group communication to be temporally continuous, spatially slow-moving and traditional in regard to textual and performance characteristics.[5] On the other hand, folklorists have abundantly documented the fact that any kind of folklore performance, whether it be of a ballad, folktale, or gesture, exhibits variation and change—hallmarks of the folklore process.[6] Conversely, the geographically expansive "spatial bias" of mass media has imbued their artistic contents with temporally discontinuous and contemporaneous qualities of the new and the fashionable. Yet, as popular culturists such as John Cawelti and Horace Newcomb have clearly shown in their formulaic analyses of westerns, mysteries, adventures and soap operas, such genres not only exhibit "inventions" (dynamism) but repeated "conventions" of form through time (conservatism).[7]

With regard to the functions of folklore and popular culture, both operate as organizational modes of activity in a social order, in that they serve to structure and provide repeatable expressive forms for individual and group experience in everyday life. In other words, they offer a means of rendering experience intelligible and graspable through recognizable forms that are both pleasing aesthetically and relevant in a social interactional sense. Tom Burns' suggestion of the role and function of mass leisure and entertainment applies readily to a similar dimension of folklore. He states:

Like ritual, it domesticates the unattainable and the threatening and reduces the increasing range and strangeness of the individual's world to the synthesized, rehearsed and safely repeatable form of a story, documentary, a performance, a show. The structures of leisure exist as repositories of meaning, value and reassurance for everyday life.[8]

Folklore and popular culture, then, can be regarded as elements of the human disposition to ritualize and order experience in stylized but substantive forms. As communication, folklore and popular culture function within—to borrow James Carey's definition—"a ritual view of communication: communication ... viewed as a process through which a shared culture is created, modified, and transformed."[9] In this way, they both constitute not only a means of communication, but also a means of generating and representing commonality through ritualized, conventional, recurrent, or traditional acts and behaviors.

The performance characteristics, media of transmission, texts and contexts of artistic communications combine in complex and intriguing ways. Several examples will be cited here. The first illustration derives from childlore, a well documented area of folklore-popular culture amalgamation. Iona and Peter Opie report in their *The Lore and*

Language of Schoolchildren many games, rhymes and songs which name such familiar screen celebrities as Charlie Chaplin, Shirley Temple, Betty Grable, Roy Rogers and Marilyn Monroe.[10] Although the Opies' young informants may never have seen any of these personalities, the lore based on these Hollywood stars has been maintained in the oral tradition of their small groups. Similarly, comic strip characters have influenced the childlore of Newfoundland. First syndicated in 1930 by Murat "Chic" Young, *Blondie* has spawned this counting-out rhyme:

> Blondie and Dagwood went downtown,
> Blondie bought an evening gown,
> Cookie bought a new pair of shoes,
> Dagwood bought the *Daily News*,
> In the *Daily News* he read,
> Close your eyes and count to ten.[11]

While on the subject of comic strip characters and Newfoundland folklore, it is interesting to note that *Bringing Up Father* or *Maggie and Jiggs*, first syndicated by George McManus in 1913, has affected Newfoundland foodways nomenclature. Thus, one of the province's favorite meals—the boiled dinner—is often referred to today as a "Jigg's dinner" in keeping with that character's penchant for the major ingredients of beef and cabbage.[12]

The colloquial associations of the term "folklore" with the old and the antique have often led to the stereotyping of the subject itself in products of popular culture—a phenomenon which European folklorists have labeled *folklorismus*.[13] *Folklorismus* is apparent in yet another folklore-popular culture conflation from Newfoundland. Advertising in Newfoundland during this century has stereotyped and mediated cultural heritage and "folklore" into what Paul Mercer and Mac Swackhammer have described as "static, quaint possessions of a rural underdeveloped populace." Their description of television beer advertisements in the province during 1977-78 is revealing in its portrayal:

Male actors, all bearded and dressed in casual work clothes are placed in situations described as traditionally Newfoundland or attached to places significant in Newfoundland history and folklore. All make use of the local legend and story-telling tradition, retelling parts of narratives collected from oral tradition. Two of the actors are popularly known to be supporters of Newfoundland culture in other professional capacities. All the scripts delivered in vernacular jargon and dialect, dwell on the advertising catch phrase, "Dominion Ale, a Newfoundland tradition."[14]

Corporate advertisers have utilized the television medium here to communicate with potential consumers through "folklure."[15] The narratives employed stem from actual oral traditions but are substantially altered and are only partially presented. While an attempt has been made to recreate some aspects of story-telling contexts, authenticity is clearly subordinate to the overall economic purpose of selling beer through entertaining video. In achieving this goal, however, regional pride in heritage is evoked. The effectiveness of this technique is not to be minimized, for the slogan cited, as well as the accompanying description, "the old smoothy with the hearty flavour," have captured the imagination of Newfoundland audiences and are often heard today as drinking toasts in small groups.

The small group use of both a mass medium and its content is evidenced in "rapping with the iron pimp"—the use made of jukebox music in narrative performances at an urban black bar. As Michael J. Bell reports:

> ...listening intently to Billie Holliday sing "Hello Heartache," Jimmy declared, "you know, when you hear Diana Ross sing that song it's nice, but when Billie sings it, you see her standing in a doorway, and it's three a.m. in the morning, and she's wearing one of them yellow kimonos, and it's half open, and she ain't wearing her hair, and she's looking up at this dude and you know she ain't too sure she's happy to see him but she don't want him to go away again. And she's sleepy-eyed looking at him and she sort of smiles and says . . . ." At this point, the record which has been backgrounding this declaration reached the final line of the song and Billie sang "hello heartache, sit down" to finish the rap. The rest of the patrons nodded with satisfaction and began a general discussion of male-female relationships.[16]

In this case, the small group traditional activity of patrons "rapping" in a neighborhood bar has become a multi-media (sensory and technological) event. The ambience for the event is provided by a musical recording which is contextualized by a narrator who times his performance in such a way as to allow the vocalist the last word.

A final instance of the commingling of small group and mass societal traits of artistic communication is the "Rocky Horror" cult, a phenomenon which has become a true contemporary ritual. The film version of the British horror rock musical written by Richard O'Brien was a commercial failure during its first months of distribution in 1974. In April, 1976, however, the midnight showings of the movie at the Waverly Theatre in Greenwich Village, New York City, launched the international cult which is still characterized by the regular attendance of a predominantly teenage audience that dresses in costumes approximating those of the movie characters. Fans anticipate, mock, and echo the actions and dialogues of the actors, and become involved in situations depicted in the film through literal enactment (e.g., throwing rice during the opening wedding scene, spraying water and opening umbrellas during a rainstorm sequence). Much of this repetitive and formulaic behavior has developed from spontaneous acts and "wisecracks" which over time have won mass collective recognition. While this cultural scene is perhaps best understood as a public or assembly event rather than a small group performance, face-to-face, sensory interaction is an integral aspect of its enactment. As Jonathan Rosenbaum has observed, "this audience, rather than allow itself to be used as an empty vessel to be filled with a film-maker's grand mythic meanings, has been learning how to use film chiefly as a means of communicating with itself."[17]

These examples demonstrate that the variables of artistic communication within the folklore-popular culture continuum can only be interpreted on the basis of case studies and that is the approach which the majority of the authors in this book have taken. The particularistic perspectives of these analyses reveal how small group and mass contexts of communication interface and parallel each other in critical ways, and accordingly, each essay contributes toward a theory of the folklore-popular culture process.

Martin Laba formulates the beginnings of such a theory in his opening essay "Popular Culture and Folklore: The Social Dimension." Laba considers the social reference group, its network and styles of communication, and its interpretive/participatory relationship to media materials as essential to defining the folklore-popular culture process. Specifically, he regards those expressive activities surrounding popular culture products as folkloric, and fundamental in analyzing the meaning and import of those products.

In direct contrast to such monopolistic mass media as the Hollywood film industry, network television and international wire services, the relatively recent development of communication forms like the cassette sound recording, the Polaroid photograph and the video cassette join a growing number of popular technological media which lend themselves to small group production and programing, and the privatization of culture. The complex performances of local "open line" shows convene the older small group electronic medium of the telephone with the mass medium of the radio. As Martin Lovelace's essay "Gossip Rumor, and Personal Malice: The Rhetoric of Radio Open Line Shows" reveals, this multi-media conflation produces an intimate format of public presentation which gives the moderator a unique and powerful role in community affairs. The small group use of the technological medium of photocopying in Canadian "photocopy lore" is revealed by Paul Smith in "Communicating Culture; or, Can We Really Vocalize a Brownie?" to exemplify his central subject—the degree to which tradition itself can be considered in terms of sensory media experience.

Peter Narváez is also concerned with media and tradition, especially in regard to radio broadcasts. In "Joseph R. Smallwood, 'The Barrelman': The Broadcaster as Folklorist" Narváez argues that Smallwood's use of the radio for the collecting of folk narratives, as well as his effective broadcast performances of traditional tall tales, resulted in a personal popularity which eventually assisted in the launching of a political career that would make him the "last living father" of Canadian Confederation. Narváez's analysis of " 'The Newfie Bullet'—The Nostalgic Use of Folklore" describes how an aural experience of the past was developed by the creators of a Newfoundland radio drama series through their use of folklore within a set of conventions particularly tailored to the radio medium. Moreover, it is shown that the resulting nostalgia fulfilled a specific mythic predilection in contemporary Newfoundland culture.

Michael Taft's study of the best-selling Newfoundland record "Aunt Martha's Sheep" focuses on the role of traditional aesthetics in popular culture.[18] He demonstrates that the song is rooted in local song-making activity, reflects well-known traditional themes and is a humorous exoteric sentiment which makes fun of mainland Canadians. Jim Hornby's article, "Rumors of Maggie: Outlaw News in Folklore," also deals with a humorous Canadian recording, one which was briefly communicated to mass audiences but which quickly entered the stream of oral tradition in small group performances because of its scandalous content regarding a Prime Minister's wife. Through this example, he develops the view that the aesthetics of popular culture and folklore are often beyond the boundaries of acceptable normative behaviour and reflect an "outlaw" quality which individuals use for their own vicarious identity voyages.

Two articles in this volume offer contextual perspectives. Robert S. McCarl's "Occupational Stereotype, Technique and the Critical Comment of Folklore," centers on the nature of popular stereotypes and the ways that the subjects of stereotypification respond to images of themselves. A specialist in the area of occupational folklore, McCarl draws from his fieldwork experience with fire fighters to depict a situation in which the members of a small group use popular culture materials for their own ends. Gerald L. Pocius is another folklorist who is interested in the uses made of popular culture materials in their social and cultural contexts. In "Holy Pictures in Newfoundland Houses: Visual Codes for Secular and Supernatural Relationships," Pocius scrutinizes the uses of popular religious artifacts in Newfoundland houses and finds that pictorial religious themes are regularly associated with the specialized social functions of various parts of a home.

In the final essay, Neil V. Rosenberg combines a production-of-culture approach with an extensive inquiry into performers' relationships to changing audiences. The useful model he refines in "Big Fish, Small Pond: Country Musicians and Their Markets" is an incisive interpretation of the complex social dimensions of folklore and popular culture.

It becomes evident from reading this compilation of essays that folklore and popular culture are interdependent categories of cultural activity in modern society. Making sense of the codes, messages and mechanisms of the folklore-popular culture continuum provides us with great insight into the nature of everyday life—our manner of interpreting and evaluating our experience, the development of our attitudes and beliefs, and the bases of our aesthetic actions.

Notes

[1]The articles by Martin Laba, Robert McCarl, James Hornby, Neil V. Rosenberg and Martin Lovelace have developed from papers initially delivered at the session on "Folklore and Popular Culture" at the annual meeting of the Folklore Studies Association of Canada, London, Ontario, June 1978. The second essay by Peter Narváez is a revised version of a paper read on the "Popularization" panel at the annual meeting of the Folklore Studies Association of Canada, Ottawa, Ontario, June 3, 1982. Three other approaches to folklore and popular culture are Joseph J. Arpad, "Between Folklore and Literature: Popular Culture as Anomaly," *Journal of Popular Culture*, 9 (1975), 403-422; Donald Allport Bird, "A Theory of Folklore in Mass Media: Traditional Patterns in the Mass Media," *Southern Folklore Quarterly*, 40 (1976), 285-305; Tom Burns, "Folklore in the Mass Media: Television," *Folklore Forum*, 2 (1969), 90-106. For a descriptive classification of regional folklore derived from popular culture see Philip Hiscock, "The Mass Media in the Folk Culture of Newfoundland: A Survey of Materials in the MUN Folklore and Language Archive," *Culture and Tradition*, 8 (1984), 20-38.

[2]The association of contemporary popular culture with the expressive culture of the mass media is common. For example, see Paul M. Hirsch, "Social Science Approaches to Popular Culture: A Review and Critique," *Journal of Popular Culture*, 11:2 (1977), 401-413; Michael R. Real, *Mass-Mediated Culture* (Englewood Cliffs, N.J.: Prentice-Hall, 1977), p. 14.

[3]This definition of folklore coincides with that of Dan Ben-Amos, "Toward a Definition of Folklore in Context," *Journal of American Folklore*, 84 (1971), 3-15.

[4]Russel B. Nye, *The Unembarrassed Muse: The Popular Arts in America* (New York: Dial Press, 1970), p. 420. Another inclusive image of the arts is Ray B. Browne's "flattened ellipsis, or lens" in "Popular Culture: Notes Toward a Definition," *Popular Culture and Curriculum*, Ray B. Browne and Ronald J. Ambrosetti, eds., (Bowling Green, Ohio: Bowling Green University Popular Press, 1970), pp. 3-11.

[5]See Harold A. Innis *The Bias of Communication* (1951; rpt. Toronto: Univ. of Toronto Press, 1972).

[6]Folklorists have developed various methodologies for dealing with folklore variation. "The Finnish method" or the "historic-geographic method" is one such approach. See Kaarle Krohn, *Folklore Methodology* (Austin, Texas: American Folklore Society, Univ. of Texas Press, 1971).

[7]John G. Cawelti, *The Six-Gun Mystique* (Bowling Green, Ohio: Bowling Green University Popular Press, 1970), and *Adventure, Mystery, and Romance: Formula Stories as Art and Popular Culture* (Chicago: Univ. of Chicago Press, 1976); Horace Newcomb, *TV: The Most Popular Art* (Garden City, New York: Anchor Press/Doubleday, 1974).

[8]Tom Burns, "A Meaning in Everyday Life," *New Society*, 9 (1967), 762.

[9]James W. Carey, "Communication and Culture," review article, *Communication*

Research, 2 (1975), 177.

[10]Iona and Peter Opie, *The Lore and Language of Schoolchildren* (Oxford: Oxford Univ. Press, 1959).

[11]Special thanks to Geraldine Burke, Long Harbour, Placentia Bay, Newfoundland, for this item. See Rolf Wilhelm Brednich, "Comic Strips as a Subject of Folk Narrative Research" in *Folklore Today: A Festschrift for Richard M. Dorson,* Linda Degh, Henry Glassie and Felix J. Oinas, eds. (Bloomington, Ind.: Indiana University Press, 1976). Comic books have also influenced childlore. See Sylvia Grider, "Media Narra-forms," in "The Supernatural Narratives of Children" (unpublished Ph. D. dissertation, Indiana University, 1976), pp. 345-450.

[12]Pamela J. Gray, "Traditional Newfoundland Foodways: Origin Adaptation and Change" (unpublished M.A. thesis, Memorial Univ. of Newfoundland (1977), pp. 16-61.

[13]See a special issue on tourist *folklorismus, Zeitschrift fur Volkskunde* 65:1 (1969).

[14]Paul Mercer and Mac Swackhammer, " 'The Singing of Old Newfoundland Ballads and a Cool Glass of Good Beer Go Hand in Hand': Folklore and 'Tradition' in Newfoundland Advertising," *Culture & Tradition,* 3 (1978), 35-45.

[15]"Folklure" was coined by Priscilla Denby in "Folklore in the Mass Media," *Folklore Forum,* 4 (1971), 113-121.

[16]Michael J. Bell, "Running Rabbits and Talking Shit: Folkloric Communication in an Urban Black Barr" (unpublished Ph.D. dissertation, Univ. of Pennsylvania, 1975), p. 111. Bell has published a different form of this "profiled rap" in *The World From Brown's Lounge: An Ethnography of Black Middle-Class Play* (Urbana: University of Illinois Press, 1983), pp. 136-37.

[17]Jonathan Rosenbaum, "The Rocky Horror Picture Cult," *Sight and Sound,* 49 (1980), 78-79.

[18]The question of traditional aesthetics in popular culture is also addressed by Gerald Thomas in "Other Worlds: Folktale and Soap Opera in Newfoundland's French Tradition," *Folklore Studies in Honour of Herbert Halpert: A Festschrift,* Kenneth S. Goldstein and Neil V. Rosenberg, eds. (St. John's: Memorial University of Newfoundland, 1980), pp. 343-351.

Popular Culture and Folklore:
The Social Dimension

Martin Laba

POPULAR CULTURE has been conceptualized in various theoretical analyses, case studies and historical treatments devoted to it as a matrix of symbolic forms established and situated through technological means, and disseminated over numerous and varied audience contexts.[1] These factors of symbolicity, technology and dissemination are further qualified by the realm of human cultural activity—the social action of individuals and groups as they identify, integrate and legitimate their experience in everyday life by making sense of and meaning from the symbolic forms of popular culture. In this way, popular culture is inextricably tied to social practices, and in particular to those practices by which social groups respond to certain material conditions of life. A folkloristic perspective of this concept points to an interface between the "countless variety of materials and ideas" that comprise popular culture,[2] and the interpretation of these materials and ideas through a parallel and responsive structure of communication—human expressive behavior.

One of the persistent problems in the analysis of popular culture has been its definition as "mass culture," a concept which critics have belabored since the nineteenth century. Attacks have originated with both right and left ideological viewponts, have reflected both literary and socio-political orientations, and have employed both aesthetic and anthropological definitions of "culture." From the approach of Leavisite literary criticism, which argued that the commercial creation of culture for mass audience consumption and market profit rendered popular art trivial and a cultural form without authenticity,[3] to the Marxist critical theory of the Frankfurt School on the nature and inevitabilities of a mass culture which ultimately served the "social function of reconciling people to bad conditions and thus diverting them from criticism,"[4] popular culture has been conceptualized as a negative social and ideological influence.

The Leavisite and Marxist approaches, indicative of European intellectual attitudes of the 1930s, were impelled by the increasing pervasiveness of American popular culture in Europe. Both the form and substance of American popular culture became factors in European

9

consumer goods and marketing strategies to the extent that America itself became "the object of consumption, a symbol of pleasure."[5]

Mass culture presented a formidable problem for American analysts as well, and as Simon Frith has noted, it became irretrievably connected to American democratic philosophy:

In the thirties, when American intellectuals agonized over joining the Communist Party and the New Deal sponsored People's Art, the dominant left ideology was a populism that found authenticity in mass culture and attacked the elitism of high art .... By the nineteen-fifties the position was reversed. It was the left ... who denounced the mind-numbing trivia, the philistinism , the debilitating political effects of mass culture, and the right, pluralists and defenders of America's cold-war honor, who proclaimed the democracy of popular culture, its wealth of choice, its enriching and educational effects.[6]

The treatment of popular culture as "mass" culture clearly dichotomizes the structures and processes of popular culture—production-consumption, industries-audiences, commodities-cultural forms, the determining factors of economics, politics, class—the "mediating realm of the human and cultural."[7] Yet any treatment of popular culture as simply a mode of material production, and predictable and reductive within that mode, is short-sighted at best. Paul Willis warns that it cannot be assumed that cultural forms are determined as an automatic reflex by macro-determinations: "Just because there are what we call structural and economic determinants it does not mean that people will unproblematically obey them."[8] The implication here is that there is a relative autonomy of processes in the cultural realm, and that structural and economic determination must be understood in relation to the quality and patterns of audience response and interpretation. The social dimension of popular culture then, is one of its most critical defining principles, and the social organization of, and relations within particular groups can be essential to the meaning-making process of certain popular culture forms. Consider the following example.

Two elderly ladies who operate a newsstand in downtown St. John's, Newfoundland, close their store every weekday from 4:30 p.m. to 5:30 p.m. to watch what is widely known in Newfoundland as "the story," the television soap opera "Another World." Customers coming into the store after its re-opening at 5:30 inevitably hear interpretive reviews of the developments in that day's episode in the often impassioned exchanges between the two women and their friends, who drop by specifically for this discussion. The event most obviously functions as a type of benign gossip, but more importantly, the event has become customary—a procedure has been established for the shaping and re-shaping of content through an active participation in an interpretive process, the discussion. In discussion the character of particular forms of popular culture may be crystallized through the verbal exchanges of the audience, and at the same time, the views and feelings of the audience members are formulated.

Tarde, and later Shibutani have argued that in dialogue vague notions transform into particular attitudes and actions, and that public opinion is invariably shaped in those discussions that occur on the local level.[9] Through a dialogue involving both verbal exchanges and a framework of customary behaviors and occasion, the two proprietresses of the news-stand and their friends interpret the content of a television show. A literal transaction is involved. Each participant contributes and takes a certain amount of information needed to synthesize her personal notions into definite attitudes, and eventually a group consensus is reached. Discussion then, in terms of popular culture is an interpretive transaction among individuals which involves a customary content and pattern of interaction. Vague notion is translated into expressive action through the ritual of the discussion event, and in this process the mass medium is framed by the context and manner of face-to-face exchange.

Clearly, customary behavior within a group both informs and is informed by popular culture. Beyond the content under discussion, there is a custom and organization to the discussion event itself. In other words, popular culture materials are supported and interpreted by a repeatable form of exchange—in essence, a social ritual—by which individuals work through and sustain their common tastes and identities in relation to those materials.[10] This ritual of exchange constitutes the social dimension of mass communication, and involves the social interactions of the individuals of a group organized around a form of popular culture. This type of "social reference group" can be understood as fundamental to the popular culture process.[11]

Individuals act in a social frame of reference as they orient themselves to particular groups. The "referent power"[12] of a group resides in the manner in which group norms, standards and perspectives become, through normative group processes, individual norms, standards and perspectives. For a group that is organized on the basis of a form of, or activity surrounding popular culture, it can be stated that popular culture itself largely molds group perspective. Shibutani postulates an equation between reference group and perspective, and defines "perspective" in a way to suggest that it provides for the individual, an orderly and predictable response to experience:

A perspective is an ordered view of one's world—what is taken for granted about the attributes of various objects, events, and human nature. It is an order of things remembered and expected as well as things actually perceived, an organized conception of what is plausible and what is possible; it constitutes the matrix through which one perceives his environment.[13]

The structures of popular culture mediate that "order of things" and form a critical part of that perceived environment. They provide reference, and therefore perspective for experience in everyday life. It is through the social reference context that popular culture commodities are made meaningful as expressive culture. The following model illustrates this process.

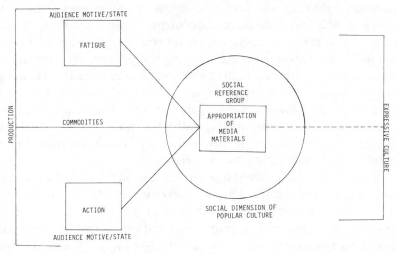

Making Meaning: From Commodities to Expressive Culture

The production of media items and activities, as represented in the figure, frames the response factors: the motive/state of fatigue and the motive/state of action. Fatigue suggests a psychological-physical state of reception which is characterized by a non-active relationship to media materials. These materials are still appropriated—stupefaction is not a concomitant of a non-active stance—and must be at least congruent with life-experience insofar as they appeal. The content of those materials appropriated through fatigue may emerge finally in the exchanges within the social reference group. Action on the other hand implies a conscious and purposeful manipulation of media materials in an active relationship to those materials. Taping music onto a blank cassette, phoning in on an "open-line" radio show, writing a letter to the editor of a newspaper, the active involvement in the taste conventions of a musical style, are all examples of the action motive. Meaning, however, is not simply a reflex of appropriation.

The nature of popular culture to be consensual, commonly approved and endorsed within audience groups is a consequence of the interpretive and participatory relationship that a social reference group establishes with popular culture productions. Media content for example is shaped in the social dimension of mass communication. Media-based popular culture materials in Figure 1 move into the sphere of influence—taste, attitude, value and experience—that is the social reference group, and are appropriated within this social context. Content is rendered manageable and meaningful as rituals of consumption and interaction become focused around certain media materials. Shared affinities for a popular culture form develop that form as an expressive vehicle, and in this way commodities produced commercially are re-produced in the social life of the reference group.

The social reference group constitutes a "culture area" bound not by territory or group membership, but by "the limits of effective communication."[14] This reference group/culture area establishes in relation to media materials an expressive culture or systems of communicative knowledge which act as expressive resources in everyday life, and which, as demonstrated by the model, frame and support the group.

Clearly, this argument for approaching popular culture in terms of its social aspects suggests a shift in perspective away from "the mechanics of communications systems" to human communicative acts in everyday life.[15] Accordingly, as Kreiling has noted, we can look to "the changing and fragmented expressive actions of contemporary life—fashion, leisure activities, popular culture—as expressive forms in which people enact patterns of sentiment, meaning and identity."[16]

Media materials may serve a given function within a group, and at the same time may be creatively handled by that group. Studies of youth subcultures, most notably those analyses in the tradition of the Birmingham Centre of Contemporary Cultural Studies, have demonstrated that popular culture objects can serve the identity and style of a group, and that the group re-interprets and re-orders these objects to suit its needs.[17] These subcultural groups are characterized as,

...cultures of conspicuous consumption—even when, as with the skinheads and punks, certain types of consumption are conspicuously refused—and it is through the distinctive rituals of consumption, through style, that the subculture at once reveals its "secret" identity and communicates its forbidden meanings. It is basically the way in which commodities are *used* in subculture which mark the subculture off from more orthodox cultural formations.[18]

In particular, these "rituals of consumption" are defined as *"bricolage,"* a concept adapted from Levi-Strauss' treatment of how, in the response of the primitive mind to the physical world, magical modes of belief and practice operate as coherent systems of homology and analogy between the order of nature and the order of society. The consequence of this process is a classification of connections which responds to, and structures the environment, and whose constitutive elements are made up or "improvised" into combinations to create new and various meanings within the classification.[19] In its application to a theory of the nature of youth subcultures to work through class concerns in the material and dramaturgical force of style, *bricolage* becomes the re-ordering and re-contextualization of an object from an established context of meaning into a new context of meaning to communicate a completely different message. This process involves the transformation of an item from an existing market of commodities into a subcultural artifact. Punk-based fashion, re-workings of popular musical idioms of the recent past (ska, rockabilly, rhythm and blues, for examples), Bob and Doug McKenzie catch-phrases entering vernacular tradition, the elaborate ritual surrounding the "Rocky Horror Picture Show," are all variants of this transformation process and demonstrate the role and significance of the audience group in such transformations. In the recurrent and ritual exchanges in the small group audience context, the item of popular culture may take on a meaning and function apart from the intention of the original producers of that item.[20]

The multiplicity of reasons for differences in the meaning and function of particular items within an audience ranges from cultural to personal bias. An example from my research into children's bawdy and parodic songs deals with a case in which age played the vital role in determining the difference in meaning of an advertising jingle for three separate groups: children aged ten to twelve years, a group of university students, and a group of middle-aged parents. The McDonald's jingle inspired laughter in the children who thought of the parody they sang at school regarding the suspect quality of the hamburger meat and the inevitable consequence of food poisoning after the ingestion of one of those hamburgers. The university students considered the same jingle as an example of ideological domination, while the parents expressed no definite feeling about the jingle, or its possible symbolic value. "Meaning," then, is not simply intrinsic to media content, but depends on whether that content has some function in relation to group attitudes (the university students), or whether it can be creatively handled by the group (the school children). A single set of media materials has the capacity to serve a vast number of audience functions. As McQuail, Blumer and Brown have stated, "One man's source of escape from the real world is a point of anchorage for another man's place in it."[21]

An understanding of the relationship between popular culture and folklore depends upon a recognition of the critical social dimension which has been defined and analyzed here. Perhaps the most evident point of connection lies in the definition of the term "popular" itself. Raymond Williams has noted that throughout the history of its use, "popular," derived from the Latin *popularis* (belonging to the people), expressed both positive and negative value:

There were neutral uses such as North's "more popular, and desirous of the common peoples good will and favour" (1580) (where popular was still a term of policy rather than of condition), and evidently derogatory uses, such as Bacon's "a Nobleman of an ancient Family but unquiet and popular" (1622). *Popularity* was defined in 1697 by Collier as "a courting the favour of the people by undue practices" .... A primary sense of "widely favoured" was clear by 1C18 [Williams' abbreviation for the last period of the eighteenth century]; the sense of "well liked" is probably C19 [nineteenth century]. A 1C19 [last period of the nineteenth century] American magazine observed: "they have come ... to take popular quite gravely and sincerely as a synonym for good." The shift in perspective is then evident. *Popular* was being seen from the point of view of the people rather than from those seeking favour or power from them. Yet the earlier sense has not died. *Popular culture* was not identified by *the people* but by others, and it still carries two older senses: inferior kinds of work ... and work deliberately setting out to win favour; ... as well as the more modern sense of well-liked by many people.... The recent sense of *popular culture* as culture actually made by people for themselves is different from all of these; it is often displaced to the past as *folk culture* but it is also an important modern emphasis.[22]

The eighteenth century use of "widely favoured," the nineteenth century emphasis on "point of view of the people," and the contemporary concept of "culture actually made by people for themselves" all point to a social basis in the definition of popular culture, and to the interface between popular culture and folklore. Qualifying remarks concerning the nature of folklore in modern society are needed to understand this interface.

The tenet of tradition is as problematic as it is crucial to the concept of folklore. Roger Abrahams has stressed some "ironic inconsistencies" in the established conception of folklore as traditional lore of the homogeneous community. The assumption of this conception is that traditions of expression are generated and sustained by only those communities which exhibit a "deep sense of common purposes and values." Yet, as Abrahams argues, those expressions that are most characteristic of a commonality of community are found as frequently, and in comparable numbers, in groups of a more casual nature.[23] Abrahams' argument accomplishes an important shift in focus and definition from the equation of lore with the traditional, homogenous community to the possibility of lore in the commonplace and casual interactions in the heterogeneous and complex social organization of contemporary urban life. The notion of "tradition" then must take on a broader meaning and application to come to terms with those casual types of groups.

The term "casual," however can be somewhat misleading. It is better understood in its reference to intent and motive rather than the nature of commingling in everyday life. Goffman, who provides the summative statement on the organization of face-to-face interaction, suggests that "when persons engage in regulated dealings with each other, they come to employ social routines or practices, namely, patterned adaptations to the rules"; that is, "ground rules" for self-expression in contact with others.[24] Abrahams offers a similar view of the rule-oriented basis of casual exchanges: "In such situations, the participants share expectations and existential state, and bring with them rules more or less in common with regard to how to handle the situations and encounters that grow out of the situation."[25] Exchanges structured by popular culture involvement tend to exhibit this casual nature, indicative of the ephemeral and commercially-generated character of popular culture, yet may involve "regulated dealings" based on established and long-term relationships (as in the case of the soap opera devotees). Folklore in each case arises as an expressive resource and interactional strategy in everyday life. It represents a continuity of knowledge and perspective, not necessarily in its content, but in its practice. A social reference group will demand or evolve its own adaptive patterns of response for usual interactional situations encountered in relation to popular culture, and folklore defines those patterns of response as they become "traditional."

Wolfram Eberhard's description of contemporary storytelling in Taiwan offers an example of this "social practice"-concept of folklore, as well as the folklore-popular culture affinity.[26] In his historical-comparative, functional and performance analyses of the content and context of a traditional storytelling event, Eberhard outlines the manner in which popular culture materials are utilized in a folkloric occasion. Modern-day storytellers use printed texts from popular heroic novels as their sources. The printed form of the text is regarded as temporary or preliminary, and is re-shaped and edited to the specific needs of the occasion. Eberhard's study leads to a logical premise: the folkloric quality of an event is not determined by the content of the verbal text—a text may be traditional or non-traditional—but by the distinctive use that the participants make of that text. "Use" in this view suggests a customary application of a text to an equally customary social occasion.

When popular culture is conceptualized as a socially-based structure of symbolic forms and human activities, it can be approached not as a product of technology *per se*, but of the various human interactions, expressive resources and patterns of communication that support and are framed by involvement in the popular culture process. The essential

connection between folklore and popular culture is in the social sphere—
the impulse to, and ways in which meaning is made by people in relation
to the more or less determining material conditions of life in modern
society. The social practice of folkloric communication is structured by the
symbolic forms in popular culture and serves as a means by which
individuals and groups ritualize, organize and make sense of those forms of
their day-to-day experience.

Notes

[1]See for examples: C.W.E. Bigsby, ed., *Approaches to Popular Culture* (Bowling Green,
Ohio: Bowling Green Univ. Popular Press, 1976); Mike Brake, *The Sociology of Youth
Culture and Youth Subcultures* (London: Routledge & Kegan Paul, 1980); Ray B. Browne and
Ronald J. Ambroseti, eds., *Popular Culture and Curriculum* (Bowling Green, Ohio: Bowling
Green Univ. Popular Press, 1972); Tom Burns, "A Meaning in Everyday Life," *New Society*, 9
(1967), 760-762; John G. Cawelti, "The Concept of Artistic Matrices," *Communication
Research*, 5 (1978), 283-303; John G. Cawelti, "Notes Toward an Aesthetic of Popular
Culture," in *Popular Culture and the Expanding Consciousness*, ed. Ray B. Browne (New
York: John Wiley, 1973).

See also John G. Cawelti, *The Six-Gun Mystique* (Bowling Green, Ohio: Bowling Green
Univ. Popular Press, 1970); Simon Frith, *Sound Effects: Youth, Leisure and the Politics of
Rock 'n' Roll* (New York: Pantheon, 1981); Dick Hebdige, *Subculture: The Meaning of Style*
(London: Methuen, 1979); Albert Kreiling, "Toward a Cultural Studies Approach for the
Sociology of Popular Culture," *Communication Research*, 5 (1978), 240-263; Bernard Waites,
Tony Bennett and Graham Martin, eds., *Popular Culture: Past and Present* (London: Croom
Helm, 1982); Paul Willis, *Profane Culture* (London: Routledge & Kegan Paul, 1978).

[2]Jack Nachbar, Deborah Weiser and John L. Wright, eds., "Introduction," in *The
Popular Culture Reader* (Bowling Green, Ohio: Bowling Green Univ. Popular Press, 1978),
p. 5.

[3]See C.W.E. Bigsby's review of the mass culture critiques, "The Politics of Popular
Culture," in Bigsby, pp. 3-25.

[4]Theodor W. Adorno quoting Max Horkheimer, in *Prisms*, trans. Samuel and Shierry
Weber (London: Neville Spearman, 1967), p. 109.

[5]Frith, 1981, p. 46.

[6]Simon Frith, "Rock and Popular Culture," *Socialist Revolution*, 7 (1977), 99.

[7]Paul Willis, *Learning to Labour* (Westmead, England: Saxon House, 1977), p. 171.

[8]*Ibid.*

[9]Gabriel Tarde, *L'Opinion et la foule* (Paris: Felix Alcan, 1901), pp. 63-158, and
Tamotsu Shibutani, *Improvised News: A Sociological Study of Rumor* (Indianapolis: Bobbs-
Merrill, 1966), pp. 129-162.

[10]See Irving Lewis Allen, "Talking About Media: Everyday Life as Popular Culture,"
Journal of Popular Culture, 16 (1982), 106-115.

[11]The term "reference group" was first applied in the field of social psychology by
Herbert H. Hyman in his analysis of the process of status. In particular, this term suggested an
individual's conception of his own position relative to other individuals; that is, an
individual's frames of reference. See Herbert H. Hyman, "The Psychology of Status,"
Archives of Psychology, 269 (1942), 5-38, 80-86.

[12]I have borrowed this term from John R.P. French and Bertram Raven, "The Bases of
Social Favor," in *Studies in Social Power*, ed. Dorwin Cartwright (Ann Arbor: Univ. of
Michigan Press, 1959), pp. 150-167.

[13]Tamotsu Shibutani, "Reference Groups as Perspectives," in *Readings in Reference
Group Theory and Research*, eds. Herbert H. Hyman and Eleanor Singer (New York: The
Free Press, 1968), p. 105.

[14]Tamotsu Shibutani, "Reference Groups and Social Control," in *Human Behavior and Social Processes*, ed. Arnold M. Rose (London: Routledge & Kegan Paul, 1962), p. 136.

[15]Eric J. Leed, "Communications Revolutions and the Enactment of Culture," *Communication Research*, 5 (1978), 305. Leed is particularly critical of the "fixation" upon the "media," and technology in general, in communication studies, and urges a reorientation to emphasize the sociocultural imperatives "which integrate a medium of communication into a given milieu."

[16]Kreiling, pp. 246-7.

[17]See for example, Stuart Hall and Tony Jefferson, eds., *Resistance through Rituals* (London: Hutchinson, 1976).

[18]Hebdige, pp. 102-3.

[19]Terence Hawkes offers a detailed and comprehensive treatment of the concept of *"bricolage"* in *Structuralism and Semiotics* (Berkeley: Univ. of California Press, 1977), p. 51.

[20]This notion is developed by Frith, 1977,

[21]Denis McQuail, Jay G. Blumler and J.R. Brown, "The Television Audience: A Revised Perspective," in *Sociology of Mass Communications*, ed. Denis McQuail (Harmondsworth, England: Penguin, 1972).

[22]Raymond Williams, *Keywords: A Vocabulary of Culture and Society* (New York: Oxford Univ. Press, 1976), pp. 198-9.

[23]Roger D. Abrahams, "Towards a Sociological Theory of Folklore: Performing Services," in *Working Americans: Contemporary Approaches to Occupational Folklife*, ed. Robert H. Byintgon, Smithsonian Folklife Studies, No. 3 (Los Angeles: California Folklore Society, 1978), p. 22.

[24]Erving Goffman, *Relations In Public: Microstudies of the Public Order* (New York: Basic Books, 1971), p. x.

[25]Abrahams, 1978, p. 22.

[26]Wolfram Eberhard, "Notes on Chinese Story Tellers," *Fabula*, 11 (1970), 1-11.

Gossip, Rumor and Personal Malice:
The Rhetoric of Radio Open-Line Shows

Martin Lovelace

RADIO "OPEN-LINE" SHOWS present a unique fusion of two media, radio and telephone. Their natures contrast and have social and psychological factors in the relationship between the mass media and their audience.

If we adopt Marshall McLuhan's conception of media as "extensions of man" we are made aware of radio and telephone as extensions of our auditory and vocal abilities; they are non-visual and hence independent of the "visual organization of experience" which McLuhan saw as being the consequence of literacy.[1] Both media are "cool" in McLuhan's usage, in that they are low in definition, involving only one sense, and thus enforce a high level of participation from the listener in order for him to complete his perception of the communication; he considered that both "involve people in depth."[2] Both offer immediate contact. There are differences in degree of participation necessary to each medium, however, and as McLuhan noted, "Unlike radio . . . [the telephone] cannot be used as background . . . [it] is a participant form that demands a partner . . . ."[3] Radio can also offer a sense of intimate communication between broadcaster and listener but such is an assumed intimacy and an imitation of social interaction. Perhaps the most important difference between the two media is that the radio broadcast is public and the telephone is private. The odd contradiction between these two aspects of the respective media contributes to the interest of these programs as does the contrast between the unpracticed communicational style of the callers and glibness of the host; the calls, via the telephone, which as McLuhan said we cannot ignore, seem heightened in reality by their situation in the vaguely unreal context of a radio broadcast.[4]

These innate characteristics of the separate media also have social consequences; thus it may be possible to speak of a form of exhibitionism and corresponding voyeurism by caller and listener as being involved in the radio broadcasting of personal conversations. Also of social significance is the phenomenon of listeners' perceptions of radio as an intimate communication directed to themselves and their response with behavior that is appropriate to a real social interaction.

The a-literacy of radio and telephone, and the immediacy of their communication, throws the forum of the open-line show open to people of all ages, social classes and levels of education, and, in the spatial dimension, allows people from a wide area to participate. Unlike the "Letters to the Editor" page of a newspaper there is no requirement of literacy and unlike a query to an advice column the response can be given immediately; the effect is to enfranchise members of a generally lower social class. This is not to say that such shows necessarily enfranchise everyone; the liberal middle class is conspicuous by its absence, a fact lamented by some United States commentators who have seen the open-line shows dominated by right-wing extremists because of the failure of liberals to participate.[5]

Another characteristic which derives in part from the nature of the radio medium itself is the creation of a "mosaic" effect in which a hierarchy of significance in events is dissolved so that all appear on the same level; thus when a celebrated actress murders her lover in Nevada and is given a minimal sentence it is discussed next to the scandal of a drunken policeman in St. John's, Newfoundland. The programs bear out McLuhan's observation that radio "contracts the world to village size, and creates insatiable village tastes for gossip, rumor and personal malice."[6] The expression of rumor is central to talk shows and Allport and Postman's sense of rumor as serving to explain and relieve emotional tensions felt by individuals through locating scapegoats and sharing fears is particularly relevant to their function.[7] Such social concomitants of this linking of two media are taken up in more detail following a short history of this type of program.

The original idea for such a fusion of the two media may be traced to initial public attitudes to telephone and radio as they first appeared. McLuhan records the New York *Daily Graphic*'s portrayal, in 1877, of "The Terrors of the Telephone" as providing a platform for political oratory and mass propaganda.[8] A similar misapprehension of function can be seen in the way that radio was first seen as a replacement for the telephone until it was realized that the public nature of broadcasting, and the proliferation of users, would make this impossible. The party line system in small communities lent itself to the organization of "programs" of communal participation which prefigure local radio broadcasting in general and open-line shows in particular; this is shown in the following account of telephone use in rural America at the turn of the century:

The *Drover's Journal*, published in Nebraska, printed the statement: "No modern invention has so thoroughly revolutionized rural communities, as the telephone."

When mail carriers could not get through local editors read the news over the telephone. "Discussion periods" were also held. Neighbors living miles apart shared "sings" and talent of various kinds over the telephone; fiddle music was the most popular. Listeners commented after each number and requested selections. Occasionally a subscriber owning a phonograph played recordings, and announced the title of his record. Thus, request programs, announcers and "canned music" were introduced on rural telephone lines, long before the advent of radio broadcasting.[9]

McLuhan also commented on the degree of "heated participation" in argument made possible by a party line and, in what seems to be his only comment on open-line shows, called them "a glorified form of the old trunk-line wire-tapping."[10]

The date of the first radio open-line broadcast is unknown; Jessica Mitford, in the best article I have seen on these shows, published in *Harper's Magazine* in 1966, puts their origin in the early 1950s.[11] Long John Nebel's night show in New York was entering its fifteenth year in 1970, according to Margaret McEachern's survey of these programs,[12] and Bas Jamieson of St. John's claimed during one of his shows (March 1977) to have been involved with open-line broadcasting for eighteen years. *Time* Magazine reports an open-line show in San Francisco in 1962 which developed from a record program in which the disc jockey heaped scorn on the records he played and then debated with listeners as they called to complain.[13] A number of articles in *Time, Newsweek, Saturday Review*, and elsewhere during the 1960s and early 1970s testify to the popularity of these shows and their establishment in this period as regular radio programing throughout North America.[14]

Open-line programs are one of the best examples of the reorientation of radio as a result of competition for the mass audience by television. Between 1948 and 1954 radio became a markedly depressed industry in the United States following the introduction of television.[15] Gilbert Seldes has described radio as a "mass-minority medium" and this perception is important in understanding the function that radio has annexed for itself in distinction to television.[16] Thus, during the 1950s, radio stations ceased to attempt to compete for mass evening entertainment audiences and concentrated on daytime community service stressing local news, weather, road conditions and local advertising. The flexibility and immediacy of radio makes it particularly well suited to this role; McLuhan also noted radio's shift from an entertainment medium to a "kind of nervous information center."[17] The open-line show is presented in this context of public service; the moderator is expected to provide information and advice on anything from emotional problems to dealing with bureaucracy.

Seldes has described some of the requirements for radio programing as including the repetition of a standard form, adding only small new elements to provide an illusion of freshness, and the making of each individual program as easy to forget as possible.[18] This repetition is sought by advertisers and the principle of "forgettability" reduces pressure to provide new material. There are also social psychological functions that are served by routine and familiarity in radio programing and some of these are discussed below. The open-line show fulfills radio's ideal with its merger of a regular format, using a familiar host, and having the creative effort to provide new material provided free by the other news media, which the host cannibalizes, and by the audience themselves in their phone calls. Most important, its apparent attention to the mood of the community accords with radio's claim to serve the public.

Public response to open-line shows may first be approached by considering attitudes to radio in general. Verling C. Troldahl and Roger Skolnik's investigation of the meaning of radio to its listeners found that its major function was of "companionship," firstly in the home but also as a portable medium. It was also felt by their respondents to provide "worldly awareness" and to create a "pleasant environment."[19] Frank L. Riggs has noted the use of radio as a "pacing factor" in the lives of its listeners who may use the regular timing and sequence of programs to structure their daily pattern of behavior.[20] Of particular relevance to the public reception of open-line show is Skolnik's study of "Alienation and Attitudes toward Radio," which emphasizes the "companionship" dimension of radio for those listeners whose feelings of alienation cause radio to become a surrogate for normal social intercourse.[21] The work of Donald Horton and Richard Wohl on "Mass Communication and Para-Social Interaction," referred to by Skolnik, is particularly apposite; their analysis of the rhetoric of television programs describes the development of a persona who speaks directly to the audience, fostering an illusion of direct personal communication through language and the ampified signification of gesture made by the electronic media in which, for example, a camera close-up on a performer enhances the sense of intimacy expressed through a literal coming closer.[22] In the para-social relationship entered into by the viewer or listener with the media persona he regards him as "friend, counselor, comforter, and model"; the persona also has the advantage of seeming stable and predictable: "his character and pattern of action remain basically unchanged in a world of otherwise disturbing change."[23] Of course the situation of the open-line shows allows *real* interaction between audience and media persona but many of the factors of idealization still apply to the relationship simply because of the glamor and authority represented by the medium as a whole.

Two radio open-line shows are currently presented in Newfoundland;

both are broadcast on weekday mornings between nine and eleven o'clock. Their titles, "Action Line" and "Hot Line," are conventional for the genre and are expressive of basic ideas of their character and purpose; it may be remembered that the telephone system linking the White House with the Kremlin during the Kennedy-Khruschev period was termed a "hot-line" with the implication that it would be used for momentous personal interventions which would defuse crisis situations. "Action line" as a term expresses a similar idea about the use of the telephone as an invocation of instant authority. McLuhan's sense of the way the telephone can "by-pass all hierarchical arrangements" is most relevant to the impression fostered by the programs that a call from the host, to the right person, can get the required "action" for listeners beset by bureaucratic bogeys.

While the program titles are oriented to electronic media the term "moderator" seems to be derived from the town meeting tradition of early America in which a moderator was always elected to supervise the conduct of the debate. The role of the open-line moderator, however, at least as intepreted by the two St. John's hosts, goes much beyond this neutral, umpire-like function and their expression of their own opinions and strong projection of personality is a vital part of their expected role.

The programs I recorded offered a number of examples of public perceptions or assumptions about the nature of open-line shows and the role of a moderator. The projection of personality is clearly important; one caller, a visitor from Ottawa, complimented one moderator on his show and gave an appraisal of an Ottawa talk show host which may reflect a general public evaluation of a moderator's expected performance:

Caller: He's got a good program, and he tells people off, he's not very shy, he lets 'em know what he thinks too!
Moderator: Oh well I have to do that from time to time you know!
Caller: I guess you do.
Moderator: (laughs).[24]

The powerful personality of the moderator, and often "the more opinionated the better," is reported from other open-line shows: a *Time* feature quotes a San Francisco host as saying, "On the radio, on the telephone, I am God," and mentions another who may tell a caller to "go gargle with razor blades."[25] It may be that some listeners are attracted to an adversary figure.

Jessica Mitford's article on open-line shows quotes a program producer who screens callers before they are put through to the moderator and uses this process to frighten or anger them and thus to stimulate them to a more lively debate on the air.[26] Few of the callers in the shows I listened to were hostile, however, for most of their aggression was directed at the various scapegoats designated by the moderator.[27] It seems likely that both moderator and callers are identified with by those who do *not* call and who "wish they had said" some of the things expressed on the air.

Both shows are punctuated by advertisements for local and national companies. A large proportion of the advertisements on one station's hot-line show are delivered by the moderator himself; he makes personal endorsements of the products and the very lack of distinction between what he says in the persona of a moderator and what he says as an advertiser must make his advertisements particularly effective for the aura of omniscience and authority is carried over from the first role into the second. In one program a caller described her troubles with a used car she had bought; she told the host that as he had started talking about used cars this was a good opportunity for her to bring up the subject of her own car. In fact the moderator had been delivering a commercial for a used car dealer but this listener had not perceived a distinction between advertising and editorial matter in the show. This effect does not occur on the rival's program where all advertisements are taped and distinct.

Nevertheless, the way that these shows juxtapose generally critical remarks about government, unions and other concerns of the day, with the uniform praise for business that is presented in advertisements causes the medium's message as a whole to be heavily commercial. This observation is based on Kenneth Burke's remark that "businessmen compete with one another by trying to *praise their own commodity* more persuasively than their rivals, whereas politicians compete by slandering the *opposition*. When you add it all up, you get a grand total of absolute praise for business and grand total of absolute slander for politics."[28] Thus while the *content* of open-line shows is political slander and human problems their effective message, highlighted by this misery and conflict, is that all is happiness, honesty and efficiency in the world offered by the advertisers. This effect is underlined in the contrast between the slickly orchestrated advertisements and the jagged voice tones of querulous or angry callers.

The sense of personal interest in each caller expressed by the moderator is an element in the appeal of the shows. One host enhances the sense of relationship by using personal names: "Good morning, John," or, "We have Mary on the line there," and this gives an air of friendship while also preserving the anonymity which makes for freedom of expression. There are many regular callers, however, for whom the programs have become a part of their everyday social interaction. Horton and Wohl, at the conclusion of their study of "Mass Communication and Para-Social Interaction," suggest that it would be valuable to investigate the truism that mass media personalities are "part of the lives" of their audiences and to "learn in detail how these para-social interactions are integrated into the matrix of usual social activity."[29] The role of the talk shows in combatting loneliness is alluded to in several of the popular articles and there seems little doubt that there are callers who rely on this fleeting and tenuous link with a sympathetic listener as their only available source of friendship.

A call to one of the St. John's shows illustrated the web of social contacts centered on the show; the caller was an elderly woman who expressed her gratitude for "the wonderful people that have been calling me and two ladies visiting me. It makes such a difference to know they like you." She asked the host if she could read a couple of little poems; a woman had called her, she said, and told her: "You didn't ring up the open-line this morning, I was so disappointed because I look forward to hearing from you." In this case the caller had clearly become something of a personality in her own right, an effect which has been noted in other shows, and the program was an occasion for her own social contact with the moderator, a chance to perform, and a means of communication with her circle of friends attracted to her via the radio show. During the same program another listener asked for her phone number as she wished to get the words of the poem.

Some callers ask to speak privately to the moderators after the show; they always agree to this and give out another number at which they can be reached. Horton and Wohl have noted that some fans attempt to transcend the limitations of the para-social relationship by actually meeting their idols and it may be that, in similar fashion, a private telephone call to the media persona gives a sense of greater intimacy and heightens the sense of solace received. A form of self censorship may also be involved here with callers feeling that their problems are too sensitive to be discussed in public. Similarly, they may be worried that the protection of anonymity will be lost in a small city like St. John's, or even more so in the outports, small rural communities, where neighbors may recognize their voices or their particular circumstances. A moderator opened one show by reporting one such private call in which he had spoken to a woman for over an hour about her recognition that her son was mentally backward; she found it impossible to communicate with her husband about it and had turned to the talk show host:

She got quite upset about the whole thing, upset to the point that she was almost hysterical when she called me and didn't know which way to turn. Well, of course she's not *alone* because there are many many children who are mentally backward .... We put it out to you, there must be many in our audience who have come up against this particular problem .... Your experience might just help this lady.[30]

The recognition and treatment of backward children became the theme of the program and many calls were received, some, as he suggested, from people who had shared this experience. While one might say, cynically, that the moderator shrewdly recognized a theme of wide appeal in this woman's concern it is also likely that the calls were genuinely helpful to her.

The parallel between the content of open-line shows and that of soap operas has been noticed by Jessica Mitford and others.[31] The similarity of their appeal may lie in the possibility of vicarious participation in other people's lives; in other words both types of program offer the chance to speculate on what it might be like to experience the various situations, such as divorce, adultery, alcoholism and other problems, portrayed in them. Horton and Wohl have described soap opera as "an interminable exploration of the contingencies to be met with in 'home life'," and suggest that it is used as instruction in appropriate roles:

In this culture it is evident that to be prepared to meet all the exigencies of a changing social situation, no matter how limited it may be, could—and often does—require a great stream of plays and stories, advice columns and social how-to-do-it books.[32]

It seems likely that open-line shows, by addressing common problems, serve in the same way by providing a stock of advice on appropriate behavior in a multiplicity of situations.

Following McLuhan's approach to media and the social effects of their inherent qualities we may observe that the open-line show as a medium fosters an unrealistic idea of political process; referring to the settlement of some political issues the moderator said, "it will be late today before we can get an answer on that," thus implying that the political process was akin to making a call on a telephone and getting an answer. The clash between the expectations of immediate action fostered by the show, as a fusion of two media characterized by instant contact, and the slowness of political procedure, was shown vividly in the uncomprehending rage with which callers on both shows responded to the news that their unemployment checks were being held at the post office because of strike action by postal workers and could not be brought out across the picket lines. In McLuhanesque terms it seemed to be a classic instance of confrontation between the rigidity of print-oriented authority on both sides, government and union, while the would-be recipients had all the fluidity and instantaneity of the electronic media through which to make their protests.

Listeners exposed to debate via radio and telephone expect political questions to be solved with the same speed: "I can't see why the head of the union is not on the radio at this time," said one caller; the pace and incorporative effect of radio communication has come to be seen as the norm for public life.

The ostensible *raison d'etre* of open-line shows is to offer democratic expression of public opinion. McLuhan was, as usual, almost right when he claimed that radio allows the realization of Plato's ideal city state which was limited in size by the number of citizens who could be in sound of a public speaker.[33] The telephone line, in theory at least, completes the circle to offer the intimate decentralized relationship of a small community.

The surveying of public opinion is a major feature of open-line shows. Recently one host has conducted a poll on attitudes to the legalization of marijuana and the other has enquired about the popular opinion of the post office: the latter also canvassed support for a projected march in sympathy with the sealers when their ships were to return from the ice. The parallels with newspaper "crusades" are obvious but one wonders whether the inherent impermanency and contemporaneity of radio as a medium does not doom these attempts at social action to be no more than talk. The notion of participatory democracy fostered by the medium is largely illusory; the real social function of these programs is to allow the venting of frustration at public bogey-figures but very little political action occurs.[34] Moderator Bas Jamieson ran unsuccessfully in the provincial election of 1982.

Both St. John's talk show hosts are politically conservative and ethically reactionary although their precise views are difficult to pin down. The conventional role of moderator in this type of show dictates that they should be on the side of public opinion. They present themselves as unofficial ombudsmen able to right wrongs by placing a phone call; a large number of calls are based on this public concept of their role and abilities. During a postal strike which had the effect of impounding unemployment checks, a moderator declared that if somenone gave him the authority *he* would cross the picket line and get those checks. This ideal of public action is generally representative of the public service image which local radio has adopted; the open-line host keeps the station's name to the fore by being involved in charity events and opening ceremonies for new businesses. The role of open-line moderator is continued beyond the studio.

Open-line shows, as a context for communication, should have particular interest for the folklorist and sociolinguist. It might be possible, for example, to define a typology of calls which could be seen in relation to other communicational styles within the group involved. Essentially people call to state their opinions but the form in which they choose to present them varies within certain traditional patterns; thus, a full rhetorical study would be needed to describe the progress of the following exchange:

Caller: Was you down again the post office lookin' at the bunch is on strike down there?
Moderator: Yeah (stalling, unable to pick up the caller's attitude).
Caller: Well what d'you think of them?
Moderator: (Still uneasy). Well, there's not much you can do about 'em, they're, uh, they're on strike and they want to be, so that's all you can do.
Caller: All you can do?
Moderator: Right.
Caller: (Delivering the set-piece he has been holding back to build effect). It's a job to know what country they belong to— I couldn't see nothing only hair down to their eyes. A hard looking bunch, they might be Portagees.
Moderator: (Countering with a proverb). You can't tell a man by the cut of his jib, you know, if he got long hair I don't suppose that means much.
Caller: No, but somebody should overhaul 'em, see what country they come from.
Moderator: (Laughs).
Caller: They might be fellers off a ship—wha'?[35]

A kind of verbal fencing is going on here with the caller attempting to commit the host to making a hostile remark against the strikers; when the host stalls the caller continues and elaborates his meaning. The moderator picks up the caller's nautical reference and delivers one of the colorful proverbs with which he adorns his speech. This teasing style of exchange in which the antagonist, the caller, does not reveal his intent until his protagonist has "shown his hand" is a traditional mode of argument.

Other common ways of presenting information include the narration of personal experience stories to support the speaker's contention; thus a person complaining of bad service from the post office will use memorates of Christmas cards that arrived in July as evidence. Some callers seem almost unable to present an objective opinion at all so that their entire presentation consists of personal experience narration. Open-line shows can thus offer an opportunity to study modes of argument which are no less real, or traditional, for being developed in the context of electronic media rather than in face-to-face interaction.

These shows create an unreal sense of the political process and tend to be reactionary in their political philosophy. In general it can be said that open-line shows offer a particular form of small-group interaction, in a natural context, that is of interest to folklorists.[36]

Notes

[1]Marshall McLuhan, *Understanding Media: The Extensions of Man* (New York:

McGraw-Hill Paperback Edition, 1965), p. 297.

[2]McLuhan, p. 291 (telephone), p. 295 (radio).

[3]McLuhan, p. 268.

[4]For a study of the distinct style of communication used in telephone conversations see Donald W. Ball, "Toward a Sociology of Telephones and Telephoners," in Marcello Truzzi, ed., *Sociology and Everyday Life* (Englewood Cliffs, N.J.: Prentice-Hall, 1968), pp. 59-75. Reference courtesy of Peter Narváez.

[5]See Erny Tannen, "Liberals and the Media," *The Progressive* 38 (April 1974), 11 and Robert Lewis Shayon, "Cleaning Up the Call-Ins," *Saturday Review*, 51 (Feb. 24, 1968), 56.

[6]McLuhan, p. 306.

[7]Gordon W. Allport and Leo J. Postman, "The Basic Psychology of Rumor," in Eleanor E. Maccoby, Theodore M. Newcomb, Eugene L. Hartley, eds., *Readings in Social Psychology*, 3rd ed. (New York: Holt, Rinehart & Winston, 1958), pp. 54-65.

[8]McLuhan, p. 269.

[9]Marion May Dilts, *The Telephone in a Changing World* (New York: Longmans, Green, 1941), pp. 32-33.

[10]McLuhan, pp. 268, 306.

[11]Jessica Mitford, "Hello, There! You're on the Air," *Harper's Magazine*, 232 (May, 1966) 48. I have found no academic discussion of these shows and my account of their history thus depends on articles in popular periodicals.

[12]Margaret McEachern, "The Town Meeting is Not Dead—It's Alive and Well on Radio," *Today's Health*, 48 (July, 1970), 32.

[13]"Radio: 'The All Night Psychiatrist'," *Time* (Sept. 21, 1962), 53-55.

[14]See Robert Lewis Shayon, "Points of View," *Saturday Review*, 48 (March 13, 1965), p. 122; "The Hot Hot-Line," *Time* (June 18, 1965), 52-53; John G. Fuller, "Trade Winds," *Saturday Review*, 49 (March 5, 1966), 112-13; "The Cool Hot Line," *Time* (August 23, 1968), 54-55.

[15]For an account of radio's response to television competition see Frank L. Riggs, "The Changing Role of Radio," *Journal of Broadcasting*, 8:4 (1964), 331-339.

[16]Gilbert Seldes, "Oracle: Radio," in his *The Great Audience* (New York: Viking, 1950), p. 109.

[17]McLuhan, p. 298.

[18]Seldes, p. 110.

[19]Verling C. Troldahl and Roger Skolnik, "The Meanings People Have for Radio Today," *Journal of Broadcasting*, 12:1 (1967-68), 56-67.

[20]Riggs, 335.

[21]Roger Alan Skolnik, "Alienation and Attitudes Toward Radio" (unpublished Ph.D. dissertation, Michigan State University, 1970).

[22]Donald Horton and R. Richard Wohl, "Mass Communication and Para-social Interaction: Observations on Intimacy at a Distance," *Psychiatry: Journal for the Study of Interpersonal Processes*, 19:3 (1965), 215-229.

[23]Horton and Wohl, 217.

[24]Transcript of radio program, St. John's, Newfoundland, March 24, 1977.

[25]"The Hot Hot-Line," *Time* (June 18, 1965), 53.

[26]Mitford, 51.

[27]But see a letter to the Editor of the St. John's *Evening Telegram* (March 8, 1977), 6, from Helen Porter complaining of a moderator's vituperative treatment of a caller who claimed that Waterford Hospital patients were maltreated; when the caller stated that he had been in the hospital as a mental patient the host remarked that perhaps he should be back inside. Reference courtesy of Paul Mercer.

[28]Kenneth Burke, from *Attitudes Toward History*, quoted in Paul F. Lazarsfeld and Robert K. Merton, "Mass Communication, Popular Taste and Organized Social Action," in Bernard Rosenberg and David Manning White, eds., *Mass Culture: The Popular Arts in America* (Glencoe, Ill: Free Press, 1960), 470.

[29]Horton and Wohl, 228.

[30]Transcript of radio program, St. John's, Newfoundland, March 24, 1977.

[31]Mitford, 47.

[32]Horton and Wohl, 222.

[33]McLuhan, 306-7.

[34]Paul F. Lazarsfeld and Robert K. Merton have discussed the "narcotizing dysfunction" caused by radio through inundating listeners with a flood of information; they come to mistake *knowing* about problems of the day for *doing* something about them; "Mass Communication, Popular Taste and Organized Social Action," in Bernard Rosenberg and David Manning White, eds., *Mass Culture: The Popular Arts in America* (Glencoe, Ill.: Free Press, 1960), p. 464.

[35]Transcript of radio program, St. John's, Newfoundland, March 24, 1977.

[36]A version of this paper was presented at the 1978 meeting of the Folklore Studies Association of Canada. It has benefited at several stages from the critical advice of Peter Narváez and Martin Laba.

Communicating Culture;
or, Can We Really Vocalize a Brownie?[1]

Paul Smith

STUDIES OF BOTH POPULAR CULTURE and its traditional counterpart, folklore, have, in the main, ignored the fact that a variety of media of communications are open to individuals for the transmission of cultural materials. As a result of this, not only the intricacies of the transmission of information have been overlooked but also the consequences.

That such an approach should be adopted by folklorists is perhaps not surprising. In the past it was considered by many scholars that one of the main definitional characteristics of an item of folklore was that it was *orally* transmitted.[2]

On the other hand, why students of popular culture should ignore the varieties of communication available is something of a puzzle. One reason is possibly that they view the message as being structured for a *specific medium* and so not viable for transmission by alternative means. If this is so, they should look again, for while popular culture is often *specific media oriented*, like all types of transmission of information, if the required or ideal medium is not available, alternative forms of communication can and will be utilized. Similarly, old ideas, in terms of popular culture images, can and often are reutilized as alternative media become available.

Fortunately, over the last few years the view that folklore is solely orally transmitted and popular culture is media tied has declined.[3] In its stead scholars now tend to favor an approach which incorporates a multi-media approach to the transmission and reinforcement of culture. If such an approach is to be adopted, however, we need to consider what are the varieties of media of transmission available, how do they interact and what are the consequences of their use for the transmission of cultural information.

Initially five types of media of transmission can be identified and these equate with the following sensory mechanisms:[4]

    1. Audio (ear)
    2. Visual (eye)
    3. Tactile (touch)
    4. Sapid (taste)
    5. Olfactory (smell)

31

Of these five the main forms usually utilized for communication are the audio and visual sensory mechanisms. These convey the majority of oral and visual information transmissions. The tactile, olfactory and sapid mechanisms are, however, nonetheless important in that they usually carry very special types of information often incorporating very fine detail. This then brings me to the sub-title of this paper—*Can we really vocalize a Brownie?* If we think in terms of how we can impart what a brownie is to others—initially we could describe how to make one, what ingredients to use, where to buy them, etc. We can draw one or show them one so that they will know what one looks like. However, we are still left with the problem that, with all the describing in the world, until they have touched, tasted and smelt a brownie their information is incomplete and they may mistake it for something else. Many parallels to this situation can be found in the transmission of cultural materials particularly in the fields of folk medicine and traditional arts and crafts as well as in many customs. For instance in the making of the garland for the Castleton Garland Ceremony,[5] in teaching his art, the maker uses mostly audio, visual and tactile communications. However, for the identification of certain pungent plants, such as wild garlic, that must not be used in the construction, both visual and olfactory identifications must be learnt by his assistant.

To enable us to understand better the nature and implications of a multi-media approach to communication I have set out the five media in a diagrammatic form (see Figure 1) and given relative emphasis to the frequency of media usage. This then gives us a basic interactive model from which to work.

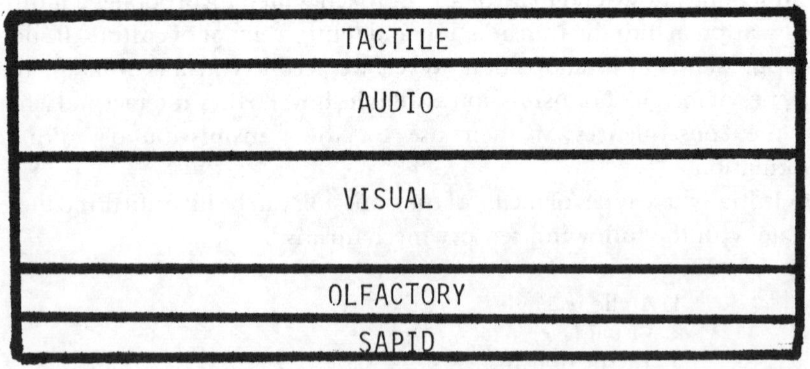

TACTILE
AUDIO
VISUAL
OLFACTORY
SAPID

Figure 1—Five Varieties of Media of Communication

It is apparent that to retain their characteristic identifiable forms items of popular culture and folklore, depending on their inherent nature, may need to utilize different proportions and combinations of these five media during transmission. One tradition may therefore utilize all the media equally (see Figure 2).

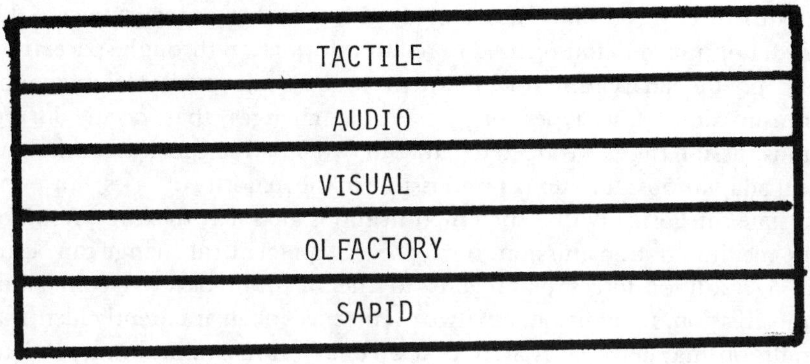

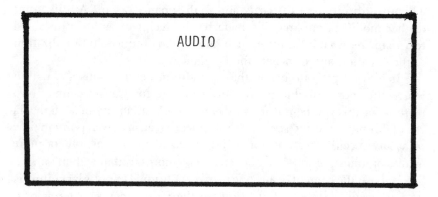

| TACTILE |
| AUDIO |
| VISUAL |
| OLFACTORY |
| SAPID |

Figure 2—Equal Use of Media of Transmission

On the other hand, another may, in theory, utilize a single medium to the exclusion of all others (see Figure 3).

| AUDIO |

Figure 3—Singular Use of Media of Transmission

Empirical[6] and experimental[7] studies of both traditional and popular culture and modes of transmission have highlighted their transitional nature in terms of the variations they exhibit through time and space. Such studies indicate that the processes involved in communication are not reliable in that rather than transmitting the information verbatim they produce a situation where the form and content of an item may become modified. This is usually the result of either the inherent inadequacy of the media of transmission utilized to retain information through space/time and/or the adaptation of the item to suit the available media of transmission. The types of irrevocable changes that occur during transmission can be grouped together in two broad categories—omissions and adaptations. It is almost impossible in the majority of cases, however, to state categorically that such modifications are solely the direct result of the medium of transmission. It may be that an identical change can occur as a result of forces extraneous to the medium or even context of transmission. In addition, any two occurrences of an apparently identical tradition may have been arrived at by totally different and independent sequences of modifications.

Although in some instances it is perhaps possible to transmit some items utilizing different combinations of media of transmission in different contexts, often certain types of information important to the reconstruction of a tradition may, as we have noted earlier, be media-bound. In such cases if the "ideal" media are not available and an alternative form of transmission has to be used, this may give rise to a situation where the media of transmission is carrying insufficient information for the recipient to reconstruct the tradition in its parent form. This in turn produces disparity and so dissonance occurs. At this point further modifications may be made by the recipient as he adjusts and revises the received informtion in an attempt to produce a rationalization of the situation and to negate the kmalancg.

It is perhaps conceivable that a tradition never attains a situation where the most suitable media are available for transmissions. Two reasons for this can be put forward. First, the availability of such media varies through time and space. This implies that at any given point in time or at any specific location, for social or technical reasons, one or more media of transmission may be relatively more available than others. Secondly, as the content of any one item of traditional or popular culture is in a permanent state of transition, so the requirements in terms of a suitable medium of transmission for that item must change accordingly. For example, there is a vast difference in the relative proportions of the audio and visual media utilized in the transmission of a simple house visitation tradition on Plough Monday, as opposed to that required to transmit the earlier more complex Plough Monday play tradition from which it developed.

It is apparent, therefore, that any initial inadequacy of a medium/media of transmission to communicate the information required for reconstruction can result not only in losses of information but also in the adaptation of the material that is transmitted. Both omissions and adaptations can be found in any part or parts of a single tradition simultaneously, as they are totally independent of each other. Where they are a product of the medium of transmission, however, as a suitable medium becomes less available and the quantity and quality of the information flow is constrained, the occurrence of these modifications will proportionately increase. In the light of this should we therefore regard all transmissions of cultural information as a possible source for the modification of culture?

It may be that only one aspect of a medium of transmission has changed or developed. Such a change may, however, have far-reaching consequences. For instance, in terms of visual communication possibly the most important development was that of movable type by Gutenberg in the 1450s.[8] This produced an increasing flow of printed literature giving authorship to traditions, ideologies, etc. which had previously formed part of the accumulated anonymous wisdom in the public domain.[9] Such a situation would imply that from 1450 onwards there has been a swing in all types of information transmission from the audio/oral to a visual/literary medium (see Figure 4).

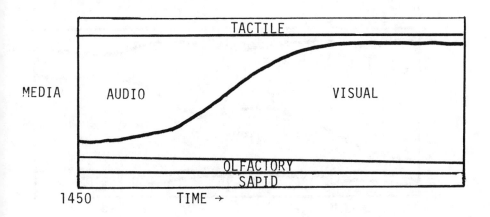

Figure 4—Change in Relative Influence of Media of Transmission since 1450

It must be remembered, however, that just because a communication is in a literary form and will consequently be able to survive transmission between two distant points or times without modification, the committing of "oral" information to a "literary" form of transmission is in itself constrained by the writer/printer's technical ability and personality.[10] However, it is feasible to consider that in relative terms specific techniques within a medium of transmission such as literature have a higher capacity for "retention" of information through transmission than others, oral communications having much shorter relative retention spans than literary ones, which also provide a point of reference for checking and re-checking. Whether such continual checking actually does take place is debatable; instead, it is conceivable that it is only in the early stages of learning a specific behavior and resulting pattern that constant reference is made to such literary sources. Such a variation in the retention of information will of course affect the resulting overall pattern of spatial and temporal distribution of a tradition.

From the 16th century onwards the annual output of printed literature increased as advances were made in printing technology[11] and literacy.[12] It was not uncommon in the early period for printers and others to put their names and imprints to printed versions of contemporary texts that hitherto had existed only in oral forms. Obviously the subsequent availability of such printed texts varied over the years, and also in different parts of the world at the same time. What occurs, therefore, is that these changes in the relative availability of media of transmission produce in our model an apparent ebbing and flowing effect over time (see Figure 5).

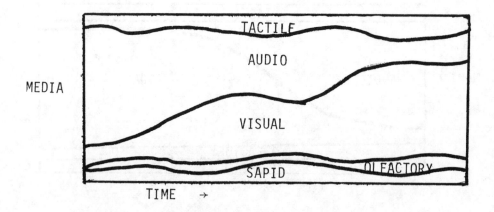

Figure 5—Hypothetical Variation in the Availability of the Media of Transmission

A change in the medium of transmission of a cultural item as alternative media become available is not uncommon, as the current work on chapbooks containing traditional play texts demonstrates.[13] One area where this is particularly prevalent today is the photocopied sheets of jokes, cartoons, parodies and narrative which circulate informally in offices and workshops and which represent a contemporary form of a tradition dating back to at least the early eighteenth century.[14] The main features of this genre which Dundes termed "Urban Folklore from the Paperwork Empire" and Preston called "Xeroxlore"[15] are as follows:[16]

1.   Such sheets exist in multiple and/or variant forms, as photocopies of text, graphic or a combination of both.[17]
2.   The sheets are essentially anonymous, though items may have a spuriously attributed author or discoverable sources.[18]
3.   Regardless of the nature of the parent document, any copies should ostensibly have been produced for "free circulation."[19]

Thematically these sheets are linked by their humorous treatment of social or cultural norms. Anti-establishment views of government and business organizations, as well as, taboos relating to excretory or sexual behavior are frequently recurring themes. This often takes the form of parody which in the case of pseudomemos is frequently associated with caustic anti-bureaucratic comment. Photocopied sheets utilizing jargon or mock-scientific terms are also frequently found circulating among clerical and technical workers.

Within these broad themes, however, the range of material occurring in the photocopied tradition is tremendous, running from philosophical poems to ethnic jokes.

Text 1[20]

No Hope, Ontario
November ......

Bank of Toronto
Ottawa Branch
Ottawa, Ontario

Gentlemen:

Just received your super heated letter in regard to the bill which I owe you. You may say that you think the bill should have been paid a long time ago and you cannot understand why it is not. I will try to enlighten you.
In 1907 I bought a sawmill on credit. In 1908 I bought an ox team and a timber

cart, two ponies, a breach loading gun, a Winchester and a $25.00 revolver. I also bought two fine razor-back hogs. All on the installment plan.

In 1910 my father died and my brother was lynched for stealing a horse. A railroad man knocked up my daughter and I had to pay $98.00 for a doctor to keep the bastard from becoming a relative of mine.

In 1911 my boy got the mumps and they went down on him and the doctor had to castrate him to save his life. That summer I went fishing and the boat turned over and I lost the biggest catfish I ever saw. Two of my boys drowned, neither being the one that was castrated.

In 1951 my wife ran away with a fat nigger and left a pair of twins for a souvenir. When I married the hired girl to keep down the expenses, I had trouble getting her to go off. I went to the doctor and he advised me to create some kind of excitement about the time I thought she was ready. That night I took the shotgun to bed with me and when I thought she was ready, I stuck the gun out the window and pulled the trigger. My wife shit the bed, I ruptured myself, and killed the best cow I ever had.

In 1938 I was burned out and took to drinking. I didn't stop until all I had left was a Bulova watch and kidney trouble. Then for some time all I did was wind the watch. The next year I decided to start over, so I bought a manure spreader, a binder and a thrashing mill. All on credit. Then along came a cyclone and blew everything into the next county. My wife got a dose from a travelling salesman, my boy wiped his ass with a corn cob that had rat poison on it, and some bastard denutted my best bull. Now at the present time if it cost a nickel to shit, I would be forced to vomit. Yet, you say that you can cause trouble for me. Trying to get money out of me would be like trying to poke butter up a wild cat's ass with a hot poker. But, Mister, you sure are G.D. welcome to try.

Text 2[21]

Lettre d'une Maman "Newfie" a son fils

NOTE — Pour le bénéfice de nos lecteurs, qui ne sauraient pas ce qu'est un ou une "NEWFIE": il s'agit tout simplement d el'habitatant de l'île Terre-Neuve. Les Anglophones s'en servent comme tête de Turc dans leurs blagues, un peu dans le même sens qu'on dit, en français, un "Habitant" ... Donc, voici le texte de cette fameuse lettre.

Mon cher fils,

Juste une ligne pour te dire que je vis toujours. J'écris très lentement parce que je sais que tune peux pas lire vite. Tu ne reconnaîtras pas la maison, à ton retour, parce que nous avons déménagé. Ca été très difficile de déménager, surtout pour le lit ... L'homme ne voulait pas nous laisser le mettre sur le taxi. Mais peut-être aussi que si ton père n'avait pas été couché dedans...

A propos de ton père, il s'est trouvé une belle job. Il a mêm 500 hommes en dessous de lui. En fait, il coupe le gazon au cimetière .... Et ta soeur s'est fiancé avec le type avec qui elle sortait. Il lui a donné une belle bague .... il n'y manque que trois pierres.

Nos voisins, les Browns, ont commencé à élever des cochons. C'est tout nouveau, nous en avons eu vent ce matin...il y avait une machine à laver dans la nouvelle maison mais je ne sais pas si nous allons la garder car elle ne fonctionne pas très bien. J'y ai perdu quatre chemises en tirant la chaîne....

Ton petit frère est rentré de l'école en pleurant hier parce que tous les autres garçons ont eu un costume neuf et lui...mais nous avons réglé le problème. Nous n'avions pas les moyens d'acheter tout l'habit alors, nous avons pris un chapeau et il reste dans la fenêtre de l'école....

Ta soeur Mary a eu un bébé ce matin. Je ne sais pas encore si c'est un garçon ou ene fille, ce qui fait que je ne peux pas te dire si tu es un oncle ou une tante. Mais ne crains rien, tout va sûrement se décider avant le baptême puisqu'il faudra lui donner un nom ....

Ton oncle s'est noyé dans un baril de whisky, la semaine dernière. Quatre de ses camarades ont essayé de le sauver mais il s'est battu bravement. Le seule incident: il voulait être incinéré et il a fally trois jours pour éteindre le feu.

Kate travaille dans un moulin à Grand Falls depuis six semaines. Je dois lui laver son linge mais ce n'est pas grand chose. Comme il lui ont fourni un uniforme en arrivant, elle ne m'envoie que ses sous-vêtements. ...

Ton père n'a pas beaucoup de boire à Noel. J'ai mis une bouteille d'huile de castor dans sa bière et ça l'a tenu occupé jusqu'au Jours de l'An.

Je suis alleé chez le médecin et ton père est enfin venu avec moi. Le docteur m'a mis un bout de tuyau de verre dans la bouche et m'a dit de la tenir fermée pendant six minutes. Je pense que ton père est jaloux car il a aussitôt décidé d'acheter le petit tube pour me le faire lui-même à la maison.

Nous avons été chanceux, il n'a plus que deux fois cette semaine. D'abord lundi puis, de mardi jusqu'à dimanche .... Nous avons reçu une lettre du croque-mort hier. Il faudrait que tu nous envoies de l'argent car il nous prévient que si nous ne payons pas la facture pour l'enterrement de ta grand-mère, il va nous la retourner. Il n'y a pas tellement de place dans notre nouvelle maison, alors ....

Je dois fermer maintenant parce que le plombier s'en vient faire des réparations et ça sent drôle.

Ta mère qui t'aime ....

P.S. Je voulais te mettre quelques sous pour ton cadeau de fêtè mais j'avais déjà fermé l'enveloppe.

This photocopy tradition cannot, however, be adequately analyzed or interpreted in isolation from other aspects of contemporary culture. There are close and constant inter-relationships between these photocopies, oral tradition and popular culture. For example, some of the material found in photocopies also occurs as commercially produced ephemera such as buttons, novelty cards and tee-shirts. A similar interaction takes place with material occurring in oral tradition. The current vogue of "Newfie" jokes has, for example, found expression in oral,[22] printed,[23] and photo-copied forms, to the extent that any of the jokes contained in *Text 3* might also be heard in conversation:

Text 3[24]

FROM NEWFOUNDLAND

The three most dangerous people in the world are: a Jew with money, a Greek with tennis shoes and a Newfie with brains.

A pimple on a Newfie's ass is a brain tumor.

The Newfie invented the wheelbarrow so he could learn to walk on his hind legs.

How about the Newfie who took a roll of toilet paper to a crap game.

And the Newfie who thought that asphalt was a rectum problem.

And the Newfie who studied for five days to take a urine test.

In Newfoundland in a recent beauty contest, nobody won.

The grocer who said eggs were 60¢ a dozen and cracked ones were 30¢ a dozen. The Newfie said crack me a dozen.

The Newfie was asked in a political discussion "What would you do with Red China?" He said it would look good on a purple tablecloth.

The reason there are no Newfie golfers, they don't know their ass from a hole in the ground.

How about the Newfie who lost his elevator job because he couldn't learn the route.

A level headed Newfie is one who has shit coming out of both ears.

It takes five Newfies to make popcorn—one to hold the kettle and four to shake the stove.

Newfies make the best astronauts—they took up space in school.

There was a Newfie who bought his wife a washer and dryer for Christmas—a douche bag and towel.

And the Newfie in the outhouse who put one leg in each hole and shit in his pants.

The Newfie who didn't believe in flying saucers until he goosed the waitress.

Doctors don't circumcise Newfies anymore. They were throwing away the best part.

What is a hula hoop—a teething ring for a big mouthed Newfie.

Newfie mothers are strong and broad shouldered from raising dumbbells.

When a man was invited to a party he said he had a case of diarrhea, the caller said, "Bring it along. The Newfoundlanders will drink anything."

Then there was the Newfie who was asked if he would like to become a Jehovah's Witness, he said he couldn't because he didn't see the accident.

Given the existence of such a common corpus of material, it is almost impossible to determine whether some of these sheets have an oral, commercially produced or "parent" photocopy source.

The existence of such material in both traditional and popular culture not only demonstrates the general appeal of this type of humor, but shows the possibility of a lengthy history of widely circulated commercial models for the form of its expression which have shaped and interacted with existing traditions.

In terms of the changing availability of the media of transmission within even this one tradition, individuals wishing a copy or copies of any particular sheet have several possible techniques at their disposal. Sheets can be copied:

1. Manually, by writing or drawing;
2. By using a combination of manual and mechanical means, such as typing, stencilling or cyclostyling;
3. By mechanical and electo-chemical processes, utilizing electric stencil duplication, photocopying, etc.

It is obvious that the majority of individuals in industrialized societies have access to some form of copying facility. The general availability of these three possible forms of duplication, however, represents a hierarchy of technology which has bearing not only on the medium of transmission but can also have considerable influence on the content of the sheets.

Copying manually or mechanically involves a complete reconstruction of the parent sheet and thus represents a laborious and relatively unreliable method of obtaining a reproduction of the parent sheet. Also, even when mechanical forms are used, duplicating a sheet might well require considerable time and effort.

Where reconstructions are necessary, conscious and unintentional changes in both the content and layout of an item can occur. A copyist may not always attempt to make a faithful reproduction of the parent sheet. The content might, for instance, be particularized by the introduction of the name of an individual or organization in what was formerly an unspecific text, or additional "applicable" material may be included.[25] Similarly, individuals trained as typists or compositors may deliberately alter the appearance of the item to accord with their training or aesthetic values.[26]

The paucity of manually and mechanically produced sheets and the overwhelming preponderance of photocopied items now in circulation suggests that the latter medium is currently the most popular form of duplication. By utilizing a photocopier, individuals can make the best use of the currently available media of transmission with minimal effort and skill, producing nearly identical multiple copies of any sheet they wish to circulate.

The implication of this situation for the tradition is, however, very important in that there is now not only a greater number of photocopy sheets in circulation but also less variation may now be present amongst the sheets sharing any one theme. The question to be posed therefore is, will the reduction in the number of variants stifle interest in the tradition or will it be replaced by an increase in the creation of new material?

Research in the area of photocopy traditions is still at a developmental stage. The studies published to date, however, effectively demonstrate that these traditions provide important examples of the contemporary function of traditional material and its inter-relationship with other aspects of popular culture.

Having illustrated the interactive nature of cultural materials and shown that they are not discrete phenomena, we must also take this interaction into account in our model.

In examining such a situation from the point of view of media influence we may find that among three cultural items, all having similar structures and functions, one increases in usage. This situation is perhaps caused by an expansion in the availability of the main medium of transmission utilized by that tradition or the decline in the availability of the media utilized by another; such a situation occurred with the printing of broadsides of selected traditional songs. Such a situation may then produce a relative decline in one of the traditions, perhaps even leading to its extinction (see Figure 6).

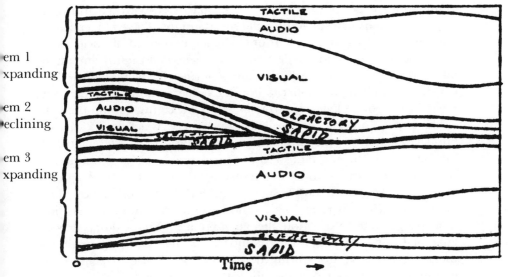

Item 1
Expanding

Item 2
Declining

Item 3
Expanding

Figure 6.

It is important also to attempt within our model to account for the development of new cultural materials. Basically these formulate when an isolated event or phenomenon is passed into a transmissional chain which continues over a period of time. Such a situation occurs when, first, a specific behavior is developed by chance or design which is considered, rightly or wrongly, to suit a particular situation. Secondly, the individual or individuals involved consider the information worth passing on to others. Thirdly, suitable media of transmission must be available to pass the information on to others. Such developing traditions possibly expand at the expense of others, but again such expansion is limited by the availability of suitable media. This situation can be diagrammatically expressed by reversing Figure 6 (see Figure 7).

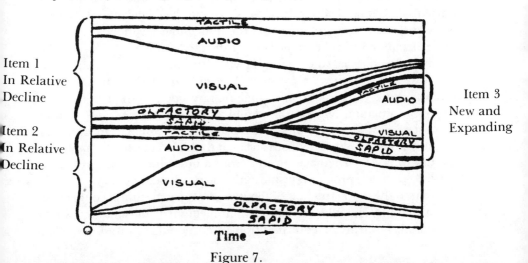

Item 1
In Relative
Decline

Item 2
In Relative
Decline

Item 3
New and
Expanding

Figure 7.

Such events happen every day, particularly in the family context. The formulation of political[27] and social attitudes[28] is easily identified as having traditions within families and social groups. There is a tendency, however, for researchers of cultural studies in industrial societies to disregard as being "non-intellectual," and therefore insignificant, many other mundane everyday tasks that are performed by the individual, like which way we hang our toilet roll on the holder or how we prepare our food. Such a point of view is surprising as for the cultural anthropologist working with "non-literate" societies—such everyday actions are his/her bread and butter.[29] Little consideration also appears to have been given to the fact that in literate industrial societies "traditions" concerning the correct way to do things and so maintain the status quo of the society group are just as strong as in "non-literate" cultures. The only difference is that in literate society there are more channels of communication reaching more people. Such a situation, therefore, produces a more homogeneous "national," and nowadays "international," culture. Within such cultures the sub-groups, far from being dependent on the mass media for the dissemination of their own specific cultural information, still rely on person-to-person communications of the sensory media type we outlined here. As communication at this level operates primarily within groups rather than between them, the selection, development and application of cultural information exhibits far more variation between groups than within them.

It is therefore within the sub-group of any society that the majority of traditional and popular culture originally develops. The extent of the eventual temporal/spatial dissemination of cultural materials depends on both the degree of contact, and so information flow, between individuals and the availability of suitable media of transmission to aid an adequate flow of information.

In summary, we can conclude that more often than not, culture, both traditional and popular, requires more than a single medium of transmission. It needs in addition, as set out in the model of multi-media transmissions above, to draw on the individual's variety of sensory mechanisms. Within the framework of the model it is probable that the audio/oral and visual/literary media will be the most commonly used. Of the two, it is practical to consider that audio/oral transmissions will produce more variations than visual/literary ones, as the latter have a higher information retention level and also provide a constant point of reference. Furthermore, the availability of a suitable medium of transmission—governed by both social and technical factors—may cause modifications to be made in the communication of culture. Such modifications are produced by the omission or adaptation of information relevant to the reconstruction of the item in its parent form. To that end, the availability and inherent nature of the medium of transmission used to communicate items of both traditional and popular culture, provide a major source for promoting variation in that culture.

Notes

[1] This paper is an expansion of my article which originally appeared as "Tradition—A Perspective: Part 2—Transmission," *Lore and Language*, II:2 (Jan. 1975), 5-14.

[2] John L. Mish, definition of "Folklore," in Maria Leach, ed. *Standard Dictionary of Folklore, Mythology and Legend*, vol. 1 (New York: Funk & Wagnalls, 1949-50), p. 401.

[3] See for example, Reiner Wehse, "Broadside Ballad and Folksong, Oral versus Literary Tradition," *Folklore Forum*, 8 (1975), 324-334; Alan Gailey, "Chapbook Influence on Irish Mummers' Plays," *Folklore*, 85 (1974), 1-22; Peter and Iona Opie, *The Oxford Dictionary of Nursery Rhymes* (Oxford: Clarendon Press, 1951); Stith Thompson, *The Folktale* (New York: Holt, Rinehart & Winston, 1946), pp. 441-2.

[4] Otto Lowenstein, *The Senses* (Harmondsworth: Penguin 1966).

[5] An outline of this ceremony can be found in G. Lester, *Castleton Garland (1972)*.

[6] Stith Thompson, "The Star Husband Tale," in Alan Dundes, ed. *The Study of Folklore* (Englewood Cliffs, N.J.: Prentice-Hall, 1965), pp. 414-459.

[7] F.C. Bartlett, *Remembering: A Study in Experimental and Social Psychology* (Cambridge: University Press, 1932).

[8] Sigrid H. Steinberg, *Five Hundred Years of Printing* (Harmondsworth: Penguin, 1974).

[9] Marshall McLuhan, *The Gutenberg Galaxy: The Making of Typographical Man* (Toronto: Univ. of Toronto Press, 1962).

[10] Liam Hudson, *Contrary Imaginations: A Psychological Study of the Young Student* (New York: Schocken Books, 1966).

[11] Steinberg.

[12] Raymond Williams, *Communications* (Harmondsworth: Penguin, 1962).

[13] Michael J. Preston, M. Georgina Smith and Paul S. Smith, "S.L.F. Research Projects: Traditional Drama. Project 1. A Classification of Chapbooks Containing Traditional Play Texts," *Lore and Language*, 1:7 (July 1972), 3-5.

[14] See Joseph Addison, *The Spectator*, Thursday, 10 May 1711, which comments that political "Accrosticks" were "handed about the Town with great Secrecie & Applause" and also notes the existence of "a little *Epigram* called the *Witches Prayer*, that fell into Verse when it was read either backward or forward, excepting only that it Cursed one way and Blessed the other."

[15] See Alan Dundes and Carl R. Pagter, *Urban Folklore from the Paperwork Empire* (Austin: American Folklore Society, 1975); and Michael J. Preston, "Xerox-lore," *Keystone Quarterly*, 29 (1974), 11-26.

[16] I would like to take this opportunity of thanking Georgina Smith Boyes and Michael Preston for not only supplying me with examples of photocopier sheets but also for their assistance and advice when structuring this section of the paper.

[17] For a discussion of this aspect of the tradition see Dundes and Pagter, pp. xix-xx.

[18] L.M. Bell, C.M. Orr and M.J. Preston, *Urban Folklore from Colorado: Photocopy Cartoons* (Ann Arbor, Michigan: Xerox University Microfilm, 1976), pp. xi-xii.

[19] Such sheets are frequently produced by a "misuse" of equipment to which individuals have access in the course of their work. It follows, therefore, that typeset and printed items produced for free transmission by such misuse also fall into this category. We have already heard of a case where workers at a Yorkshire firm of colour printers were producing copies, in up to six colors, of several items current in local photocopy tradition. Furthermore, with the introduction of offset-litho machines and IBM typewriters into commercial offices, it may in future prove difficult to distinguish which items have been produced commercially and which by "misuse" of available equipment.

[20] Original held in Memorial University of Newfoundland Folklore and Language Archive. Contributed by Laurel Doucette.

[21] Original held in the author's collection. This sheet was circulating in one of the largest Quebec provincial government office complexes during March 1976.

[22]See Gerald Thomas, "Newfie Jokes," in Edith Fowke, ed. *Folklore of Canada* (Toronto: McClelland & Stewart), pp. 142-153.

[23]See for example, Bob Tulk, *Newfie Jokes*—No. 5 (St. John's: n.p., 1979); Robert Sheppard and Edwin Noftle, *Newfie Laffs* (Lewisport: n.p., 1979).

[24]Memorial University of Newfoundland Folklore and Language Archive, 75-120.

[25]Often jokememos are typed on the headed note paper of the organization for which the typist works.

[26]As noted in J. Hartley and P. Burnhill, *Typography, Communication and Learning* (SSRC Final Report HR 1494), pp. 30-31.

[27]David Butler and Donald Stokes, *Political Change in Britain: Forces Sharing Electoral Choice* (New York: St. Martin's Press, 1969).

[28]M. Young and P. Willmott, *Family and Kinship in East London* (London: Routledge & Kegan Paul, 1957).

[29]George Murdock, et al., *Outline of Cultural Materials*, 4th Revised ed., Behavior Science Outlines, Vol. 1 (New Haven: Human Area Relations Area Files, 1961).

Joseph R. Smallwood, "The Barrelman":
The Broadcaster as Folklorist

Peter Narváez

IN AN AGE WHEN CABLE TELEVISION subscribing Canadians employ various techniques of media-mockery in order to cope with the grade "C" movie re-runs of a President of the United States who used to share star billing with higher simians, it is easy to forget that electronic media also launched the careers of prominent Canadian politicians. In particular, William Aberhart (1878-1943), the Premier of Alberta from 1935 to 1943 and founder of the Social Credit Movement, first gained a large public following through the popularity of his radio sermons. Likewise, the last living father of Confederation, the Honourable Joseph R. Smallwood attributes his major political achievement of Newfoundland's union with Canada, as well as his twenty-three year premiership of the province, to his success with a radio program—The Barrelman. This presentation will discuss The Barrelman in terms of format and content with specific reference to the ways that it functioned for listeners. In addition, it will interpret the role of Joe "Barrelman" Smallwood as folklorist and folk performer in order to shed greater light on the value of existent Barrelman program materials for the interpretation of Newfoundland culture.[1]

A one-man show dedicated to "making Newfoundland better known to Newfoundlanders" through the presentation of geographic and economic facts, historical information, and folklore, The Barrelman was aired 6:45 to 7 p.m., six nights a week, eleven months a year, October 1937 to December 1943 by government-owned radio station VONF from studios on the third floor of the Newfoundland Hotel in St. John's. With the use of re-cycled scripts, journalist Michael Harrington continued to announce the show through 1956, but the program was never more popular than when the "original" Barrelman was in charge.

Prior to the radio program, "The Barrelman" was Smallwood's signature pseudonym for a newspaper column. Having completed his editorial tasks on the two volume *Book of Newfoundland* in the Spring of 1937, Smallwood approached the Honourable John S. Currie, the editor of the *Daily News* and obtained a column entitled "From the Masthead" by "The Barrelman." Smallwood considered the title and signature of the column to be very appropriate. He explains:

The Barrelman is a man onboard a whaling ship or a sealing ship who goes up to the top of the mast in a barrel because at that altitude he can see farther and shout down directions to the skipper of passages through the ice or herds of seals or a whale or whatever they're looking for and as the Barrelman he sees farther and he sees more, you see, than anyone. So "From the Masthead," by "the Barrelman," a pretty good caption for a column, and that ran daily on the page opposite the editorial page, a very prominent place for it, and it very rapidly became an extremely popular column.[2]

In calling himself "The Barrelman" Smallwood was keeping in step with journalist fashion, for catchy pseudonyms were the style of the day— Albert Perlin in *The Telegram* was known as "The Wayfarer" and A.A. Parsons employed a pun by signing his column "R.U. Wright."

By Smallwood's own account, "From the Masthead" was a feature which "consisted of anecdotes about Newfoundland, bits and pieces and scraps of information about the country and its people, and in general was devoted to a sort of glorification of Newfoundland and everything good within it."[3]

The medium of print, however, could not compete with Smallwood's fascination for radio. He has often expressed the view that because of Newfoundland's great expanse and scattered population "God had Newfoundland particularly and specifically in mind when he brought about the invention of the radio."[4] Spurred on by the need for more lucrative employment as well as by the success of his friend Oliver L. Vardy, who was a popular radio news commentator, Smallwood submitted the idea of a Barrelman broadcast to VONF station manager and announcer William Fintan Galgay who approved a brief pilot series. Smallwood then met with a potential sponsor, St. John's merchant Francis Martin O'Leary, who listened to the show for several nights and then agreed to back the broadcast by paying the Barrelman thirty dollars a week.

The choice of Frank O'Leary as a sponsor was calculated. As a commission merchant, O'Leary had entered into a short-lived partnership with Gerald S. Doyle in 1922 and afterwards the two businessmen had become arch rivals.[5] Indeed, it was a productive competition which for three decades served the Newfoundland public well through the following parallel commercial manifestations of popular culture: in the 1920s Doyle began distributing a free newspaper throughout the island, *The Family Fireside* and O'Leary eventually countered in 1938 with the publication of Barrelman radio scripts in *The Barrelman,* a monthly tabloid newspaper which later changed its name to *The Newfoundlander*; Doyle began publishing and freely distributing paperback folksong collections in 1927 entitled *The Old Time Songs and Poetry of Newfoundland* and in 1939 O'Leary distributed "Barrelman Song Sheets" through Van Camp food products for a loose-leaf *The Barrelman Song Folio of Newfoundland*

The Barrelman
(Photo courtesy of Provincial Archives of Newfoundland and Labrador Centre for Newfoundland Studies, Smallwood Collection.)

Ballads and English, Irish and Scotch Folksongs; beginning in 1932 on VONF Doyle sponsored the most popular radio program in Newfoundland broadcasting history, the personal message-laden Doyle News, and then in 1937 O'Leary supported The Barrelman; in 1939 O'Leary briefly backed a radio program organized by the Barrelman, The Van Campers, a musical group performing "Newfoundland songs and ballads" and in 1949 Doyle attempted a Christmas broadcast of "folksongs of old Newfoundland." Joe Smallwood was always aware that in the contest of these enterprising spirits O'Leary was usually a step behind Doyle.

...you have to bear in mind the rivalry, the friendly but intense rivalry that existed between Frank O'Leary and his business competitor Gerald S. Doyle. They were both of approximately the same age, they were both in approximately the same kind of business, commission merchants, commission agents. They were both, I think, the son, each of them was the son of a sea captain, they both came up the hard way, but Gerald Doyle was a bit ahead of Frank, he got his start a bit earlier than Frank did but he was the one, he was the measuring yard, he was the yardstick by which Frank O'Leary would judge his own progress and his own success. So he always had a very keen eye. Well when Gerald S. Doyle had this news that everybody in Newfoundland is listening to, Frank perhaps would be a wee bit jealous....[6]

The format of The Barrelman radio program was straightforward. Each show began with this opening formula:

[Bell sounds six times]
Announcer: F.M. O'Leary Ltd. presents, "The Barrelman"!
Barrelman: Ladies and gentlemen, good evening...

The unique aural feature here was the bell which sounded six times at the beginning and end of each program and sounded once between each narrated item. Smallwood likens his use of the bell to the dashes in his column for the *Daily News*.

...well, there's sort of a dash between items in print. I had a bell, it was a ship's bell, in fact it came off a yacht and, I gave ding ding, ding ding, ding ding. I didn't use the clapper, that wasn't controllable, I had a glass rod and I'd attack the bell smartly ding ding, ding ding, ding ding. See! Six bells! Well that was the nearest you could get on a ship's bell to that time which was quarter to seven every night.[7]

In the middle and at the conclusion of each program one of O'Leary's products such as Pepsodent Tooth Paste, Gillette Blue Blades, Buckley's Mixture or Palmolive Soap, was advertised by an announcer or the Barrelman himself. The scripts for these advertisements were prepared by the manufacturers but sometimes the Barrelman enhanced them with his own sound effects as in the following example:

When you hear a man talk about shaving troubles nowadays it's quite certain he has not tried the "new improved" Gillette Blue Blades. They're made of steel, hard enough to cut glass [long, loud scratching sound].[8]

Smallwood's assistant Leo Moakler recalls that at one point during the program's run Joe and Frank O'Leary decided to employ a female announcer for the sake of "extra variety." The Barrelman devised a public hiring process:

With his flair for the dramatic he didn't just go into the marketplace and hire an announcer. He made it a carnival event in which his public could participate. ,Through his program he got applicants to audition at the VONF studios. Nine or ten were finally picked. Under assumed names one each week gave the O'Leary commercials. Listeners then voted for their choice. In came the votes in thousands, the winner being a St. John's girl, Miss Florence Mercer. She was to be known as "The Palmolive Girl," after Palmolive Soap.[9]

After the Palmolive Girl was selected, O'Leary and Smallwood argued over which closing tag the Palmolive girl should read, "this is the Palmolive Girl bidding you all goodnight" or "your announcer, the Palmolive Girl, bids you all goodnight." They allowed Moakler to make the final decision which he remembers as "a traumatic moment wondering which of them I would disappoint."[10] The final formula for each show from then on was:

F.M. O'Leary Ltd. will present the Barrelman tomorrow night at a quarter to seven in another program of making Newfoundland better known to Newfoundlanders. This is the Palmolive girl bidding you all goodnight. [Bell sounds six times][11]

As is the case with all media-sensitive performers, Smallwood paid close attention to the sound of his broadcasting voice. Moakler recollects:

Joe was always concerned about his style of delivery over the air. His natural style was, as it is today, the declamatory. Every now and then he would decide, or maybe someone told him, that this was not suitable for his kind of program. He would then adopt a modulated conversational delivery with not a histrionic in it. Next day, without fail, whether it was the declamatory or the conversational, I would be confronted with the inevitable question, "How was I last night?"[12]

Within a year of the initial Barrelman broadcast, VONF purchased a wire recorder and the Barrelman finally heard his own voice. Smallwood's reaction to that experience as well as his immediate use of pre-recording technique and its social consequences are revealed in this item of "media lore":[13]

I was surprised as everyone is, everyone is surprised when he first hears his own voice on a record. But I didn't mind it. I liked it and I now was able to take advantage of that system because when I wanted to go out of town say for the week, which I wanted several times each year, I would make recordings of the missing nights you see and I've had funny experiences that way. I was so well known, my program and my voice, that I remember being in a little outport on the Southern Shore in Newfoundland and they were all excited to see me because they all heard that I was the Barrelman, Mr. Smallwood, and I was at this house having dinner with them, a cup of tea and some cake and so on and suddenly the bell rang and I perked up and everybody perked up and they began listening to me. You should see the suspicious looks on their faces. Who was this imposter, who was coming pretending to be the Barrelman you know?[14]

The intended social consequences or manifest functions of The Barrelman were education, the validation of culture and amusement. The first two of these functions were inextricably linked to Smallwood's determination to rid Newfoundlanders of what he called "our inferiority complex." Although Richard Gwyn has maintained that "politics rarely intruded" into The Barrelman, Smallwood argues that in attacking the concept of inferiority head-on, the program bolstered the integrity and confidence of Newfoundlanders and, therefore, was political in the broadest sense of the term.[15]

...my program was very political, every word that I uttered for those six years, six nights a week, eleven months a year for six years, that's sixty-six months is it? Ah, I, I was aimed at stirring and creating and fanning Newfoundland patriotism, a sort of Newfoundland nationalism, I was trying to destroy the horrible inferiority complex that our people had. The minute you crossed the Gulf, everything was better going away but coming back, the minute you crossed the Gulf everything was inferior. Nothing could be as good as it was up-along, up-along to the Boston States or up-along to Ontario or Nova Scotia or somewhere, there was a terrible inferiority complex and I, by giving countless, just countless you know many hundreds of examples of Newfoundlanders displaying marvelous skill, marvelous ingenuity, marvelous originality, actual genius and then great strength and great speed and great resourcefulness and so on and so on, and so on, you know I was building, I was glorifying, I was doing the American job you know glorifying the American girl, I was glorifying every Newfoundlander, trying to make them puff out their chest and be proud and abandon this cursed inferiority complex. That was my purpose. Oh, that was a very political purpose.[16]

The pervasive theme of The Barrelman was the validation of Newfoundland culture through a focus on successful Newfoundlanders. In order to make a successful Newfoundland better known to Newfoundlanders, Smallwood endlessly culled stories of fame, fortune and achievement from the St. John's Gosling Library. Moreover, he cautiously appealed directly to his listening audience for program material concerning the accomplishments of Newfoundlanders.

You see, I am trying to show the world that Newfoundlanders are a smart people. I am trying to show that they always succeed, every time they get a decent chance. Help me to prove this, by sending me the cases you know about yourself.

Send me stories—true stories—showing how brave are the Newfoundlanders; how hardy they are; how strong they are; what hardships they endure.

There are some people, you know, who don't think very much of us Newfoundlanders. Let us prove to them that Newfoundlanders have courage, brains, strength, great powers of endurance.

Let us show them that Newfoundlanders are witty and smart.[17]

Thus, the Barrelman chronicled the achievements of such persons as: the Newfoundland ship-owner Edwin J. Duder; the heroic Captain James Dalton who fought for the Americans during the Spanish-American War; the wealthiest Newfoundland clergyman, Rev. Joseph J. Curling of Birch Cove; the oldest woman in Newfoundland, Mrs. Ellen Carroll of North River (b. 1827); Harry Watson who was a hockey star for the Toronto Granites; Captain Bob Bartlett the master mariner; and Captain George Whiteley who invented the codtrap.

Other success stories, however, featured contemporary working-class individuals such as this one about Edward Dinn:

I'm sure, ladies and gentlemen, you'll all be glad to hear that Edward Dinn, the man who walked seventy miles to town in his rubber boots, short coat and overalls to seek a berth to the ice, has landed a berth and will be going to the icefields tomorrow morning on the steamship Imogene. The broadcast hadn't finished two minutes last night before a telephone call came in, and there was his berth—I'd very much like to give the name of the gentleman who gave the berth, but I'm not permitted. And then a couple of minutes later the phone rang again, and there was a good overcoat for this hardy Newfoundlander. I didn't ask Mr. Wiseman, of Williams Street, if I might use his name, but I'm taking the chance—he's a real Newfoundlander, with a Newfoundlander's good heart. So Mr. Dinn goes off tomorrow morning with hundreds of other sturdy Newfoundland seal-hunters, and I'm sure it won't be his fault if he doesn't earn a good bill. Tonight the hearts and minds of all Newfoundlanders are with our brave and fearless seal-hunters, and there isn't one who doesn't wish them all quick voyages, bumper trips, good health and a good bill.[18]

In addition to success stories, the Barrelman aired educational historical information which furthered the validation of Newfoundland culture through instilling a sense of regional pride in heritage. This example concerning Fogo is typical:

It's just about 237 or 238 years ago since the prosperous and important settlement of

Fogo was founded. As early as 1738 Fogo had 215 inhabitants. Of these, 143 remained for the winter, the others returning to spend the winter at their homes in England. Fogo was fortified in those days, and 'twill be interesting to know if any of the old cannons are still to be found down there. A small contingent of soldiers used to be stationed in the settlement in the early days for defense, not only against the French, but American privateers around the middle of the 18th century. In 1750 Fogo was badly harrassed by those privateers.[19]

One of the most celebrated social service features of The Barrelman was The Fish Appeal during World War II. As devised by The Newfoundland Patriotic Association, O'Leary and Smallwood, The Fish Appeal was an extremely successful campaign whereby "each fisherman would donate a salt-dried codfish, and all the fish would be sold to the highest bidder; the proceeds would be used to buy cigarettes and comforts to be sent to our boys in the army, navy, and air force in Britain or wherever they were."[20] By prompting a show of solidarity in a noble cause, the Barrelman not only dramatically validated the beneficence of Newfoundlanders but also latently urged mass conformity to high ethical values. The manipulative powers of the Barrelman as salesman through his rhetorical technique of reiterative exposition are marvelously exemplified in this plea for Fish Appeal collectors.

I personally don't believe there's a person in Newfoundland today who wouldn't cheerfully contribute to The Fish Appeal. The fund is the worthiest, the most deserving cause in this country today and nobody is going to refuse to contribute. But before anybody can respond to a collection there's got to be a collection. And before there can be a collection there's got to be a collector. And every settlement that has no collector is deprived the privilege of responding to this appeal for our boys. So it's supremely important to have at least one collector in every place in Newfoundland. We want to make this the banner year of all so let's get our shoulders to the wheel and get her rolling for those boys.[21]

The popularity of The Barrelman, however, did not rest simply on fish appeals and lectures about the great achievements of Newfoundlanders, for interlarded amongst such materials were items like this:

Here's a story that's been lying on my desk for three or four weeks, buried underneath a pile of unanswered letters. It's contained in a letter sent by Mr. G. Sooley, of Prescott Street in the city, and tells about a sixteen-year-old lad named Bram Travers of Heart's Delight. I think Bram Travers must be the strongest young man in all the country. He can stand a full-sized puncheon of molasses on its head with a steady strain, and without jerking it. Two men can hold up a barrel head and he'll drive his fist through it with one blow. He struck a bull on the forehead once, and knocked him flat on the ground. He can take a five-inch nail in his naked hand and drive it through a piece of three-inch plank. He can take a fifty-six and a twenty-eight tied together, hold it over his head with his little finger, and with a pencil held in his remaining fingers write his name on the wall. He's a great swimmer and diver, and on more than one occasion he dived under and was gone so long that someone jumped in clothes and all after him, only to be fooled as two or three minutes after diving Travers would pop up several hundred yards away. The peculiar thing about this lad is that when he was five years old he was pushed into a bonfire by another boy and was burned so badly that his own mother couldn't recognize him. It was William James Reid who hauled him out of the fire and took him to a brook about six hundred yards away. Today his body doesn't carry even one mark.[22]

Without labeling such materials "folklore," the Barrelman collected and broadcast an abundance of Newfoundland oral traditions and this folkloric content provided entertainment and grass roots interest for his listening audience. Indeed, the Barrelman's efforts in eliciting narratives from his listeners were not unlike those of the modern folklore collector who: 1) conceives of clear goals for a fieldwork project; 2) makes calculated attempts to locate articulate informants, oftentimes through seeking out the key gathering places of such persons; 3) establishes rapport with informants and collects data utilizing various prompting techniques; 4) organizes, edits and analyses his collected materials. The Barrelman's collecting objective was a broad one which involved an "open-net" approach to folk narrative. That is, his goal was to amass any interesting narratives pertaining to Newfoundland, particularly those concerning remarkable incidents or memorable achievements. With regard to securing informants in key gathering places, the Barrelman had a tremendous advantage over the modern folklorist in that his program along with The Doyle News were themselves catalysts for social occasions in communities throughout Newfoundland. As Smallwood explains:

...without electricity they had to use battery sets and you'd see wind chargers all around the island, people revving up their batteries. But you also had an interesting practice that people would flock to each other's homes and take turns so as to save the battery you see. There'd be eight or ten or twelve or fifteen or twenty people crowded into the kitchens of a neighbor's house and then the next night they'd crowd into the kitchen of another neighbor and so on, and in this way they could all manage to hear the particular, not sit down all night with the radio turned on, they couldn't afford that, not with battery sets, but the things that appealed to them, that interested them. My program did, The Barrelman. The Gerald S. Doyle News Bulletin. Every last living soul in Newfoundland listened to that, to the news, to the Doyle News, which wasn't permitted soon after Confederation came because news on the C.B.C. was not permitted to be sponsored you see. And that was a sponsored newscast to which the entire population listened to. Well there were not many fewer that listened to The Barrelman. That too was an enormously popular program.[23]

The Barrelman easily gained rapport with his listening public. Not only were his amiable voice and genial manner a winning combination on the intimate medium of radio, but prospective informants were also prompted into action by material inducements, i.e., free samples of Frank O'Leary's products for writing in "any story or unusual incident likely to prove interesting to other listeners."[24] When coaxing his listeners to write in their stories, Smallwood was always encouraging and never condescending. He was especially sensitive to allaying any insecurities his listeners might have had regarding their writing deficiencies:

Don't worry about how your letter is written. I'll fix it up to suit. That's my job, and I'm only too delighted to get your letters and fix them up.[25]

Smallwood's collecting efforts yielded a great harvest. At one point in his second year of broadcasting he reported fifteen hundred letters from two hundred communities in a four month period, half of which told "a story or anecdote."[26] The folklore form which prevailed in this response was the tall tale. It was also the only genre of folk narrative which Smallwood directly appealed for through illustration. He remembers:

The first tall tales I told in my program were three of four that I had heard from my grandfather David, and he had brought them with him from Prince Edward Island. Then an avalanche descended upon me. Newfoundlanders, especially outport people, loved my tall tales, and they wrote me hundreds of tales to tell.[27]

The Barrelman's collection of tall tales exemplified virtually every major subdivision of the genre. There were tales regarding extraordinary hunting and fishing incidents, strong men and amazing physical feats remarkable vegetables, unusual domestic pets and livestock, sea serpents and incredible stupidity. Many of these stories exhibit well-known motifs and some are complete international tale-types, as the one about "the man who bent his rifle barrel in a semi-circle to kill a large number of birds grouped around the edge of a well." Whether international or native to Newfoundland, however, all of the Barrelman's tales reflected a strong regional flavor, such as this narrative about a fisherman who straddled a horse mackerel:[28]

Mr. Richard T. Cook of Cartyville says that back in 1888 a few years before the railway was put through out there, only a very little agriculture was carried on out that way—most of the people made their living at the fishery. One spring somebody reported that the caplin had struck in at the Highlands, about eight miles away. About ten o'clock that night all the fishermen took their boats and started off to get caplin for bait. Mr. Cook, then a boy of fourteen, was taken along with his father. When they got there they found it was a false alarm—there were no caplin. It was a lovely calm morning, the water as smooth as glass. They were just getting ready to turn back again when somebody shouted: "Look! Horse mackerel—look at them jumping!" Of course horse mackerel is the Newfoundland fishermen's name for tuna fish. A short distance from the shore there they were—a big school of the tuna fish, diving and sporting in the water. Hurriedly the men loaded their boats with fairly large stones from the beach and pulled for dear life on the oars. They rowed out fan-wise, to get outside of the school of fish and to form a sort of flank on both sides of them. They then began throwing the stones for all their worth at the tuna fish—the idea was to frighten the fish and make them stampede toward the beach. And that's exactly what happened—by flinging the rocks, splashing the water with their oars and shouting they kicked up a fearful din, and the tuna fish were forced in toward the shallow water off the beach. Squeezed in right against each other, the big fish began to splash and jump and dive themselves—if you've ever been present when a salmon-trap was dried up with eighty or a hundred fighting salmon, you'll have some idea of what a racket those big tuna fish would make under those circumstances. One of the fishermen in the boats was a Scotsman named John Rory Gillier perhaps it was John MacRory Gillis—he was in a boat with his brother Alex Gillis. John Gillis was poised up on the stem of the boat, and in the excitement, as one big tuna came up out of the water Gillis leaped clear onto his back, sitting astride and holding for dear life to the fish's fins, one in each hand. The startled tuna immediately began to dive and jump, and then dived clear under the water, just long enough for both fish and man to take a deep breath, and dived again. The fishermen in the surrounding boats were at first paralyzed with astonishment at the unheard-of daring and recklessness of John Gillis, but when they recovered they closed in upon the tuna and began striking it with their oars and boat-hooks till they had him out of commission. Mr. Cook doesn't say how long or heavy the tuna was, but adds the information that he was at least three if not four times as big as the man. John Gillis is still living—he's out in British Columbia. His brother Alex is still living at the Highlands in the Codroy Valley. Mr. Cook concludes by asking if anybody knows of any other man that ever rode astride on a live tuna—well, I think I can answer that for Mr. Cook: I don't think there's another man alive in the world today who can truthfully lay claim to such an astonishing achievement of sheer recklessness and daring.[29]

Occasionally the Barrelman indicated that a listener's account was a tall tale through comments such as "take this with a grain of salt," "'tis a fairly tall story." In rare instances a letter contained sufficient information to enable Smallwood not only to identify a tall tale but to present it in its performance context. This story about Newfoundland weather illustrates what one student of folk narrative has called "the best documented function of the tall tale... its use as a means of mocking the greenhorn."[30]

I image that all Newfoundlanders who have been disgusted by the peculiar ideas so many people outside Newfoundland have about this country will get a kick out of a story that one of the soldiers in our Newfoundland Regiment told an English visitor at a camp in England during the Great War. This visitor was quite curious, not only about the Regiment itself, but the country from which the Regiment came. "You have a lot of ice and snow out there, don't you?" he asked. The soldier's first instinct was to correct the impression by a simple denial—but as he thought swiftly, he figured there was a better way. So he agreed, and said yes, there was lots of ice in Newfoundland—and proceeded to tell him all about the ice. He said that the people built their homes of ice. Each family would begin building their house from the ground up, toward the sky, until the house would be 30 storeys high. Then, said he, when the warm weather comes in the summer the sun melts the house from the top storey down. In some cases, he explained, the summer was over and the melting stopped by the time it got down around the ninth or tenth storey from the ground—which meant that instead of having to build another 30 storeys they had only to build about 20 or so on top of what was left standing. By the time he got through, the visitor, at least, began to get the idea that his impression of Newfoundland's climate was a little bit astray.[31]

Another example of the Barrelman reporting a tall tale with contextual data involves the depiction of a "lying competition." Moreover, it is the first recorded public usage of the slur "Newfie."[32]

And Mr. Arthur B. Walker, of Charlton Street, sends another story to illustrate the wit of the Newfoundlander—I'm afraid it's a bit rusty by now but anyway here it is: It happened in New York, where a group of men who happened to be of different nationalities were congregated one day, a Newfoundlander being one of them. They were boasting of their respective countries, and the topic turned to feats of fast workmanship, especially in the building line. After they'd all had their say the American turned to the Newfoundlander, and remarked: "Nothing like that in your country, eh, Newfie?" "Why, that's where we have you Americans beaten to a standstill," retorted the Newfoundlander, and then, as the American demanded to know what he meant, he explained: "On my way to work at quarter to seven one morning down in St. John's I saw a crowd of workmen excavating for the foundation of a big new apartment building. At quarter past six that same evening I was returning the same way from work, and saw the tenants of that new building being turned out for failing to pay back rent!"[33]

While the analysis of tall tales was beyond the purview of the Barrelman broadcast, Smallwood did make some interesting observations regarding the genre. For instance, he believed that he had made the discovery that "if there is a distinctive type of humor that is liked more generally in Newfoundland than any other, it's the tall tale."[34] Although he never used the term "cuffer," which has been reported in some parts of Newfoundland as meaning tall tale, the Barrelman was adamant in his attempts to clarify what he considered to be the confused and erroneous usage of those listeners who referred to "tall tales" and "lies" synonymously.[35] The distinguishing features of these terms were that a lie "is meant to deceive" and a tall tale is told to be enjoyed.[36] Like all fiction, the tall tale was a form of creative literature.[37]

If a tall tale is a lie simply because it is something that never happened, then all novels, all plays, all Shakespeare's works, Dante's "Inferno," Milton's "Paradise Lost" and most other famous works of literature are lies too—which of course is absurd.[38]

Similarly, Smallwood emphasized that the differentiation of tall tales from historical truth was a simple exercise.

...a tall story is in a class to itself—there's no chance of mistaking it for anything else, whereas a true story, no matter how strange or unusual it may be, should be recognized instantly for what it is.[39]

In actuality, however, it was difficult to ascertain the degree of truthfulness of many of the narratives that the Barrelman read on the air. Often he did not corroborate his facts or cite his sources and not infrequently he even expressed doubts about the veracity of his materials with asides such as "is this true?" or "can we believe this?"[40] A few listeners warned the Barrelman that "if I go on telling tall tales people won't believe the true stories."[41] In his introductory remarks to a narrative concerning a steamship, which was elevated and lowered by an iceberg without incurring damage, he admitted to a disturbing side of his public image:

I can't help it if you refuse to believe the story I'm going to tell you now. I'm told as a matter of fact, that I'm acquiring a frightful reputation as a liar.[42]

This reputation at one point was concretely expressed in an honorary full membership in the Association of Colossal Liars and Exaggerators Amalgamated Union which was sent to the Barrelman by the Secretary of that organization, Mr. X. Aggerator of Bay Roberts.[43]

In order to understand how the Newfoundland public perception of the Barrelman as "liar" or narrator of tall tales evolved, it is necessary to view this circumstance as a combination of factors, namely, the folk view of the status and style of the tall tale teller in traditional contexts, the performance style of the Barrelman himself, and the characteristics of the radio medium in the context of the Newfoundland home during the period of The Barrelman broadcasts.

With regard to group status, folk narrative analyst Gustav Henningsen has maintained that tall tales are usually narrated by men whose occupational activities take place in settings which are sufficiently removed from their prospective audiences so as to disallow any possibility of their facts being checked upon. For this reason such groups as fishermen, hunters and soldiers possess tall tale traditions "while sedentary people who live in a community where everyone knows everything about everyone else are cut off from similar fictions."[44] The work of James C. Faris supports this thesis for Newfoundland outports where women are said to "gossip" while fishermen prod lagging conversation through the technique of the "cuffer" whereby mundane experiences are exaggerated in order to start arguments and other forms of verbal interaction.[45] Henningsen also maintains that the accomplished and highly esteemed folk narrator of tall tales has achieved his individual status through years of displaying verbal skills at various social events. Such a narrator tells his story in the first person as a reminiscence and staunchly maintains an attitude of seriousness and veracity. His posture is reinforced through the use of legend telling devices, such as the listing of circumstantial details, which lend credence to the performance. In addition, there is often a group of initiated participants in the audience who in a "cooperative tall tale telling" assist in mocking the uninitiated through a sympathetic listening.[46] It is the sustained contrast between narrative content and the histrionics of the narrator's delivery which provides the humorous dissonance of the tall tale experience.

Given these generalizations regarding tall tale performance traditions, let us imagine an outport kitchen one evening in the late 1930s in which a small group of men and women are listening to The Barrelman. The locus of the family kitchen—the room of friends and relations—and the intimate nature of the radio medium give a warm ambience to the social gathering. Everyone knows that the Barrelman is Joe Smallwood but like most media personalities he is only recognized through his public presentation of self in a few publications and on the radio. Except for the possibility of writing to the Barrelman, the listeners accept the Barrelman's communication as a serious unidirectional aural flow from far away St. John's. He is articulate, armed with facts that no one could ever check, and he seems omniscient. In fact the Barrelman is so knowledgeable that during this particular show he announces a contest whereby he will award a pound of Lyons Tea to anyone who can ask him a question of general Newfoundland interest that he cannot correctly answer. He then proceeds to narrate this story:

I wonder how many of my listeners ever knew Lemuel Rodgers, of Red Island, Placentia Bay? Back in 1907 Mr. Rodgers was on a visit to St. John's. He was in Slater's dry good store one day, and in full view of all the clerks and a number of customers he took several three-inch cut iron nails and bit them off one by one with his teeth. And if you think I'm romancing, write up to Red Island and prove it for yourself.[47]

The men in the room know a cuffer when they hear one and recognize the Barrelman as one of their own. They enjoy it and laugh. The levelling effect of the radio mosaic makes the cuffer about Lem Rodgers' teeth seem just as significant as the Barrelman's apparently serious ramblings about Governor John Holloway's treatment of the Beothuk Indians in 1805. The fact that the radio medium prevents dialogue with the Barrelman does not prevent one male participant from asserting that the Rodgers story is true. An argument amongst the men ensues after the program. Needless to say, the Barrelman that day accrues more prestige for his verbal ability to tell a cuffer and to explicate what some outport Newfoundlanders have deemed to be the real "news," i.e., "anything strange."[48]

Exaggeration, remarkable events and amazing facts were so much a part of the Barrelman that there is little doubt why Smallwood's listeners regarded him as a great raconteur of the extraordinary. Even F.M. O'Leary's products were advertised by the Barrelman in a manner which sometimes smacked of the tall tale. This point was personally dramatized for me by the Barrelman himself when immediately after re-enacting an advertisement for Buckley's Mixture he exclaimed "you see, Buckley's Mixture could cure anything!"

The importance of the Barrelman scripts and correspondence for folklorists and students of Newfoundland culture is that they represent the results of a five year folklore and oral history project by a broadcaster who amassed a tremendous amount of primary documentation which deserves scholarly analysis. Furthermore, an understanding of the folkloric content of The Barrelman would enable folklorists to assess the degree to which the program's transmission of folklore in Newfoundland modified, revived, or created new oral traditions.

In the latter regard I am reminded of a folklore survey card which was deposited by a Memorial University student in the folklore archive in 1966. The card recorded a children's expression from Grand Bank and contained an explanatory note which plainly illustrates the extent to which the legacy of The Barrelman is a part of contemporary Newfoundland folklore.

"You tells more lies than the Barrelman." This means that a person tells a good many lies, more than is usual. I have not been able to find out what or who the "Barrelman" is.[49]

The significance of The Barrelman for Joseph R. Smallwood has always been eminently clear—it made his voice familiar to Newfoundlanders and through the Confederation debates of the National Convention that familiar voice carried the day to union with Canada and his appointment as Premier. Yet, if one of the major points of this discussion is correct—that the public image of the Barrelman was that of an entertaining raconteur and tall tale narrator—it would appear in the worst interests of the Newfoundland public of the time to follow the lead of a person with a reputation as a "liar" no matter how amusing he was. Beyond being a good teller of cuffers, however, the Barrelman represented stability and consistent benevolence. Unlike problem-oriented open-line radio shows which feed on conflict, The Barrelman was perpetually informative, humorous, and success-oriented.

Moreover, in tradition-directed oral cultures, such as that of Newfoundland during the period in question, individuals who exhibit great verbal ability often command high esteem and respect. Similarly, but with specific reference to narrators of tall tales Gerald Thomas has noted:

"It has become increasingly clear that the tall tale is frequently linked with the names of individual tale-tellers.... These storytellers often become legendary characters in their own lifetime, acquiring impressive reputations as the protagonists and narrators of their own remarkable deeds."[50]

On the order of Abraham "Oregon" Smith and Gib Morgan of the United States and Larry Gorman of Prince Edward Island, the Barrelman's oral skills and traditional folklore repertoire launched a career of heroic proportions.[51] Unlike Smith, Morgan or Gorman, however, Joe Smallwood's verbal performances were transmitted by a new, awe-inspiring and intimate electronic medium into the personal lives of a widely scattered population. With the genius of a true showman who is sensitive to the desires of his public, the Barrelman created a winning formula which was well tailored to the medium of radio. Many listeners were correctly convinced that there was no one quite like the Barrelman. Perhaps a Barrelman fan, Mrs. Nath Brian of St. John's, summed up the Barrelman's appeal better than anyone.

> Dear Barrelman I send to you
> This letter that you see,
> To say we like your broadcasts,
> We hear just after tea.
> They are so very grand indeed
> To us who like to hear
> Of Terra Nova's heroes
> Come floating through the air.
> As for your advertisements,
> We think they're wise enough;
> As Buckley's Mixture for a cold
> Is for me the only stuff.
> Now may I say in closing,
> Of Newfoundlanders great or small
> Our most noted Barrelman
> Is unique among them all.[52]

Notes

[1]Reprinted from *Canadian Folklore canadien*, 5:1-2 (1983), 60-78, by permission. This article is a revised version of a paper delivered at the annual meeting of the Association for the Study of Canadian Radio and Television, June 4, 1983, Learned Societies Conference, University of British Columbia, Vancouver, British Columbia. In the preparation of this essay I have utilized the sound recordings of the

CBC radio archives in St. John's, Newfoundland, as well as "The Barrelman" scripts housed in the Centre for Newfoundland Studies (CNS), Memorial University of Newfoundland. In particular I would like to thank the following persons for the valuable assistance they have provided: Joseph R. Smallwood, Anne Budgell, Leo Moakler, Herbert Halpert, Philip Hiscock, Anne Hart, Nancy Grenville, Greg Kealey, Judy Adler, Ken Hill, John O'Mara, Roger Bill, and Gerald Horwood. My interview with Joseph R. Smallwood, August 10, 1982, is deposited in the Memorial University of Newfoundland Folklore and Language Archive (MUNFLA), Tape, 82-185/C5844.

[2]MUNFLA, Tape 82-185/C5844.

[3]Smallwood, Joseph R. *I Chose Canada: The Memoir of the Honourable Joseph R. "Joey" Smallwood* (Toronto: Macmillan of Canada, 1973), p. 205.

[4]MUNFLA, Tape, 82-185/C5844. A similar comment is transcibed in Bill McNeil and Morris Wolfe, *Signing On: The Birth of Radio in Canada* (Toronto: Doubleday Canada, 1982), p. 34.

[5]Paul O'Neill, *A Seaport Legacy: The Story of St. John's, Newfoundland*, Vol. 2 (Erin, Ontario: Press Porcepic, 1976), p. 911. For details about Gerald S. Doyle's folksong projects see Harold Paul Mercer, "A Bio-Bibliography of Newfoundland Songs in Printed Sources" (unpublished M.A. thesis, Department of Folklore, Memorial University of Newfoundland, 1978), pp. 82-89. An account of Francis M. O'Leary's enterprises is available in A.B. Perlin, *The Story of Newfoundland* (St. John's: n.p., 1959), pp. 180-81.

[6]MUNFLA, Tape, 82-185/C5844.

[7]*Ibid.*

[8]CBC soft-cut disc recording, 21A, September 10, 1943.

[9]Leo Moakler, "The Barrelman: Making Newfoundland Better Known to Newfoundlanders" in James R. Thoms, ed., *Just call Me Joey* (St. John's: Creative Printers and Publishers, 1968), pp. 18-27.

[10]*Ibid.*

[11]CBC soft-cut disc recording, 21A, September 10, 1943.

[12]Moakler, pp. 20-1.

[13]By "media lore" I refer to oral communications in which technological media occur as significant elements of content.

[14]MUNFLA, Tape, 82-185/C5844.

[15]Richard Gwyn, *Smallwood: The Unlikely Revolutionary* (Toronto: McClelland and Stewart, 1972), p. 55.

[16]MUNFLA, Tape, 82-185/C5844.

[17]*The Barrelman*, 1:1 (June, 1938), 3.

[18]CNS, Script, March 4, 1938.

[19]CNS, Script, March 25, 1938.

[20]Smallwood, pp. 207-8. See also Moakler, pp. 25-6.

[21]CBC soft-cut disc recording, 21A, September 10, 1943.

[22]CNS, Script, March 4, 1938. Pertinent motifs in Ernest W. Baughman, *Type and Motif-Index of the Folktale of England and North America* (The Hague: Mouton and Co., 1966), are: X941, "Remarkable lifter;" X945, "Lie: remarkable lifter or striker;" X945 (a) "Man kills animal with blow of hand;" X964, "Lie: remarkable swimmer;" D1841, "Invulnerabililty for certain things."

[23]MUNFLA, Tape, 82-185/C5844.

[24]CNS, Script, October 26, 1938.

[25]*The Barrelman*, 1:1 (June, 1938), 3.

[26]*The Barrelman*, 1:9 (February, 1939), 14.

[27]Smallwood, p. 207.

[28]*The Barrelman*, 1:12 (May, 1939), 20; Antti Aarne and Stith Thompson, *The Types of the Folktale* (Helsinki: Suomalainen Tiedeakatemia Academia Scientiarum Fennica, 1961), Type 1890E, "Gun barrel bent to make a spectacular shot." Another Canadian variant of this popular North American tale may be found in Michael Taft, *Tall Tales of British Columbia*, Sound Heritage Series, No. 39 (Victoria: Provincial Archives of British Columbia, Sound and Moving Image Divison, 1983), p. 51.

[29]CNS, Script, November, 7, 1938; Baughman, X1153, "Lie: person catches fish by remarkable trick;" X1004.1, "Lie: man rides unusual riding animal."

[30]Gerald Thomas, *The Tall Tale and Philippe d'Alcripe* (St. John's: Department of Folklore, Memorial University of Newfoundland for the American Folklore Society, 1977), p. 8.

[31]CNS, Script, October 29, 1937. Stith Thompson, *Motif-Index of Folk-Literature*, 6 vols. (Bloomington: Indiana University Press, 1955), X1030, "Lie: remarkable buildings."

[32]For discussions of the "liars contest" see Thomas, pp. 10-11, 26-27, and Taft, p. 11. The earliest reference to "Newfie" or "Newfy" in G.M. Story, W.J. Kirwin and J.D.A. Widdowson, eds., *Dictionary of Newfoundland English* (Toronto: University of Toronto Press, 1982) is cited from a dictionary of slang published in the United States—Lester V. Berrey and Melvin Van den Bark, comps., *The American Thesaurus of Slang* (New York: Thomas Y. Crowell, 1943).

[33]CNS, Script, March 10, 1938. Baughman, X1796.01 "Liars' contest concerning speed in skills."

[34]*The Barrelman*, 1:12 (May, 1938), 21.

[35]On "cuffer" see Story, et al., pp. 128-9 and James C. Faris, *Cat Harbour: A Newfoundland Fishing Settlement*, Newfoundland Social and Economic Studies, No. 3 (St. John's: Institute of Social and Economic Research, Memorial University of Newfoundland, 1972), pp. 148-9.

[36]*The Barrelman*, 1:9 (February, 1939), 14-5.

[37]Essentially the same distinction has been made by Chandra Mukerji in a dramaturgic interpretation of road lore tall tales. "Bullshitting: Road Lore Among Hitchhikers," *Social Problems*, 25:3 (February, 1978), 242: "When people bullshit or gossip, they do not so much tell lies as create situations where events can be elaborated in non-ordinary ways. Just as a stage play is not a lie though it takes events from life and heightens their drama to make good theater, so bullshitting takes events and heightens their story-telling possibilities."

[38]*The Barrelman*, 1:12 (May, 1939), 21.

[39]*Ibid.*, 19.

[40]*The Barrelman*, 1:10 (March, 1939), 14 and 1:4 (September, 1938), 11.

[41]*The Barrelman*, 1:12 (May, 1939), 20.

[42]*The Barrelman*, 1:3 (August, 1938), 18.

[43]*The Barrelman*, 1:12 (May, 1939), 19. For a discussion of similar associations and societies see Thomas, p. 11.

[44]Gustav Henningsen, "The Art of Perpendicular Lying—Concerning a Commercial Collecting of Norwegian Sailors' Tall Tales," *Journal of the Folklore Institute*, 2:2 (1965), 180-219.

[45]Faris, pp. 144, 148.

[46]Henningsen, 213-5.

[47]CNS, Script, October 29, 1937. Baughman, X916 (c), "Remarkable jaws and teeth."

[48]Faris, pp. 148-9.

[49]MUNFLA, Survey Card, 66-13/53. I am grateful to Philip Hisock, Archivist, MUNFLA, for bringing this item to my attention.

[50]Thomas, p. 3.

[51]William Hugh Jansen, *Abraham "Oregon" Smith, Pioneer, Folk Hero and Tale-Teller* (New York: Arno Press, 1977); Mody C. Boatright, *Gib Morgan: Minstrel of the Oil Fields* (Dallas: Southern Methodist University Press, 1965); Edward D. Ives, *Larry Gorman: The Man Who Made the Songs*, Indiana University Folklore Monograph Series, No. 19 (Bloomington: Indiana University Press, 1964).

[52]*The Barrelman*, 1:9 (February, 1939), 7.

"The Newfie Bullet"—The Nostalgic Use of Folklore

Peter Narváez

THE MATERIALS OF FOLKLORE may be strategically employed by producers of popular culture in order to prompt specific kinds of audience responses. This discussion will examine a Newfoundland radio drama series and focus on the ways that the creators of the show used folklore in order to evoke nostalgia, a bittersweet and sometimes melancholic emotional state in which an individual believes that he is re-experiencing a past situation within living memory.[1]

The radio program under consideration, "The Newfie Bullet," derived its title from the nickname of the main passenger line of the narrow-gauged Newfoundland Railway, the now defunct *Newfoundland Express*, a service which was regularly provided between St. John's and Port aux Basques from June 29, 1898 through July 2, 1969.[2] It has been suggested that the terms "Newfie" and "Newfie Bullet" were sarcastically coined by American servicemen during World War II while utilizing the *Newfoundland Express* for transit and supplies between major bases in Argentia, Botwood, Gander and Stephenville.[3] This supposition is partially substantiated by the fact that the earliest reference to the word "Newfie" in print appears to be in the 1943 edition of Berrey and Bark's *American Thesaurus of Slang*.[4] Newfoundlanders almost universally dislike the condescending use of the term by outsiders in expressions such as those found in "Newfie jokes."[5] However, many Newfoundlanders use the term esoterically with connotations of possession and endearment, and Newfoundlanders who call the *Newfoundland Express* the "Newfie Bullet" employ it in this manner.

Whatever the reasons for the usage, it is clear that the *Newfoundland Express* has often been manifested in the popular culture and folklore of Newfoundland as the "Newfie Bullet." Artifactual manifestations include such tourist items as "Newfie Bullet" cups, mugs, T-shirts, tea towels, framed photographs, place mats, gaming cards and a commemorative coin. In addition, there is a "Newfie Bullet" games arcade, a "Newfie Bullet" restaurant and even a "Newfie Bullet" cocktail.

With regard to folk compositions, three songs exist in Newfoundland oral tradition about the *Newfoundland Express* as part of the "Wabash

65

A Newfie Bullet commemorative coin (photo courtesy of Corner Brook Chamber of Commerce).

A Newfie Bullet Gaming Card

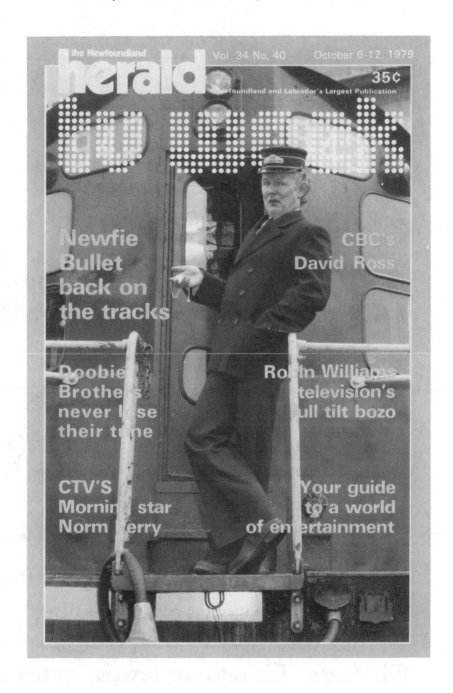

Cannonball" parodic cycle.[6] All three have been referred to as "The *Newfoundland Express,*" although one is sometimes also called "The Answer to the *Newfoundland Express.*" As is the case with the majority of other songs associated with the "Cannonball" cycle, one song is celebratory of the vehicle with lines like, "No better transport anywhere, you'll find if you would ask, as that which chugs along the line from St. John's to Port aux Basques."

Another "Newfoundland Express," however, is a satirical piece which was written during World War II by either American servicemen or by American actress Joan Blondell. Such verses as "you'll surely spoil a new suit, on the Newfoundland Express," "the fireman and engineer were drunk so I was told," "I guess I'll spend my furlough, on the *Newfoundland Express,*" lampoon the conditions, service and pace of the train. The third song, "The Answer to the *Newfoundland Express,*" is a Newfoundland response to the preceding satirical parody. It roundly rebukes the insults of foreigners:

Come all ye foreign soldiers a little while will do
To answer to those insults that was composed by you,
Ye were sent down here to guard our shores, but all ye did, I guess,
Is run down our country and our *Newfoundland Express.*[7]

It is noteworthy that the more nostalgic epithet "Newfie Bullet" does not occur in any of the foregoing songs but that it was used by the popular Newfoundland singer Michael T. Wall in his 1975 recording of his own composition lamenting the train's demise, "Ode to the Newfie Bullet."[8]

An elaborate and dramatic musical display of the Bullet's popular links with Newfoundland folklore was made several years ago when Newfoundland composer Brian R. Sexton used the train as a framework for a symphonic presentation of such well-known Newfoundland folksongs as "The Badger Drive," "She's Like the Swallow" and "I'se the B'y."[9] Entitled "The 'Newfie Bullet'—A Newfoundland Journey," Sexton's composition was given a unique perspective through the interspersion of a number of dialogues by members of Rising Tide Theatre.

Rising Tide's past connection with the "Newfie Bullet" was even more encompassing in their own successful play "Daddy, What's a Train?" which toured the province in the fall of 1978. That nostalgic work combined historical fact, story and song, and collective creation into an educational and entertaining series of dramatic sketches.

In December 1978, John Dalton, then a local producer for CBC Radio in St. John's, saw "Daddy, What's a Train?" and approached a member of the cast, actor David Ross, with the proposition of developing his role of conductor on the "Newfie Bullet" into a variety radio program. Shortly thereafter, Ross consented to write the series and play the leading role. Simply titled "The Newfie Bullet," the weekly show ran through three thirteen week runs in 1979, 1980 and 1981.[10] In its first season "The Newfie Bullet" appeared to be a radio version of its theatrical antecedent in that characterization and coherence were subordinated to musical variety entertainment and historical explanations. By the final run, however, history had been dropped, musical variety played a lesser role and the program had evolved into a nostalgic, conventionalized situation comedy.

The drama was nostalgic to the extent that through it a listener could experience a bittersweet, specially reconstructed and personalized recent past which was superior to present circumstances. The renovated past of this radio play approximates the historical myth of "Old Newfoundland," an ideational construct often embraced today by educated middle class Newfoundlanders and "C.F.A.s" (those who come from away). This myth postulates a period before the resettlement of small coastal village "outports" to large "growth centers" (1953-), or an era before Newfoundland joined the Confederation of Canada (1949), when outport life was *the* good life of family, home, and perpetual collective "times," occasions when everybody enjoyed a steady diet of foot-stomping jigs and reels, fine traditional songs, great stories, superb food, and satisfying rum. While such a mythic vision of the past is not necessarily false, the blurred outlines of this paradise lost profoundly influence the popular arts in Newfoundland and "The Newfie Bullet" is a good example of this tendency.

The use of folklore throughout the drama's run abetted the nostalgic experience and was integral to the creation of a mythic past. One folkloristic approach to such a product of popular culture as a radio program is to catalog the folklore contained in the broadcasts and pursue questions of sources, authenticity and variance.[11] Although this is a useful pursuit, it is less pertinent to an understanding of the relationship of folklore and popular culture than is the question of how folklore works with the systems of conventions which characterize popular culture forms. It is the use of folklore within such sets of conventions which shall be the focus for the ensuing examination of "The Newfie Bullet."

Popular culturist John Cawelti has developed the term "conventions" to refer to "elements which are known to both the creator and his audience beforehand."[12] Such conventions function in terms of continuity, stability and identity. As a radio variety sitcom, "The Newfie Bullet" demonstrated conventions of sound (aural), setting (scenic), characterization (personae) and dramatic action (plot).

Conventions of sound are particularly important to nostalgic radio drama because, as McLuhan perceived, the medium of radio possesses the potential to awaken "the sense of the total past as *now*."[13] Since radio imagery is the result of radio sound and the creative imagination of the listener, who must provide all the auxiliary sensory information to give the sound meaning, it is crucial that initial radio sounds be aurally inviting. With this in mind let us imagine the introduction to "The Newfie Bullet" through the scripted format:

CONDUCTOR: All aboard!
TRAIN WHISTLE:
MUSICAL THEME "Piccadilly Sand"
ANNOUNCER: The time is the early 1960s and the "Newfie Bullet" is chugging along somewhere between St. John's and Port aux Basques. Conductor Jack Foley is waiting to take your ticket, so if you're ready it's all aboard the "Newfie Bullet!"
THEME FADES, TRAIN SOUNDS BEGIN IN BACKGROUND
CONDUCTOR: Tickets please.
SOUNDS OF TICKET PUNCH.

For purposes of the following analysis the aural conventions of "The Newfie Bullet" are distinguished from the scripted dialogue and may be understood in terms of ambient noise, instrumental music and song, and linguistic categories. The linguistic category may be further subdivided into annunciatory statements, verbal formulas, oral narratives and folk speech. The overall effect of the confluence of these conventions is that they usher the listening audience into the past. In the preceding example the first aural convention to greet the listener is an item of occupational folklore, Conductor Jack Foley's stylized verbal formula "All aboard!" To regular listeners it is a friendly and totally expected welcome that is always followed by the ambient noise of the train whistle which is at once sonorous but distant. This sound is then succeeded by a traditional Newfoundland instrumental melody ("Picadilly Sand") and the overlay of an announcer's intimate invitation to the listener to get on board a train that is travelling in a vague time ("early 1960s") and in an unspecified location ("somewhere ..."). The conductor's amiable formula "tickets please" and the sound of the ticket punch assure the listener of a place of security on the train. The soft ambient rumbling of the "Bullet," heard throughout the program beneath the characters' voices, engages the listener, making him aware of a radio experience that is quite different from his normal listening habits. The sequence and convergence of these introductory conventions promotes a very positive symbolism. Historically trains have symbolized not only strength, speed, progress and escape but also industrialization, monopoly, pollution and death.[14] Yet there can be no question here that the "Bullet" represents anything but friendship, good times and the continuity of a living memory.

Following a fade on dialogue and train sounds, the ending of each show exhibited similar aural conventions, namely the annunciatory credits being read over the musical theme. In the early days of the drama the volume of the train sounds was raised and lowered in order to provide time lapses or a shift of scene. By the last series, however, the same function was served by what in broadcasting parlance is known as a "sting" or a "stab," that is, a brief instrumental interlude. The stings for "The Newfie Bullet" consisted of either the theme or some other traditional music, often played on the accordion by one of the main characters.

Of all the aural conventions used in the show, traditional music and folksong played perhaps the most obvious role in reifying the good times of the past. As one passenger put it, "music and rum, that's the 'Bullet' to me."[15] In the vast majority of the forty programs aired, at least two or three of the musical items per show were readily recognizable by the listening audience as being traditional Newfoundland melodies and songs. The two musical instruments currently associated with traditional Newfoundland music, the accordion and the fiddle provided their distinctive sounds to many of the dramas. In addition, popular traditional musicians and singers like John White, Ray Walsh, Minnie White, Emile Benoit, Kelly Russell, Ron Hynes and Pamela Morgan played the role of performer-passengers who at regular intervals would respond to the cajoling of Conductor Foley and burst into song or instrumental melody.

While such a variety format may appear ludicrous on a passenger train, the actual reminiscences of former "Bullet" patrons bear witness to such activities. For example, Victor Butler, a former resident of Harbour Buffett recalls:

After eating supper, a young man came to our seat and said, 'we are a band of musicians; we are out in the smoker. You and your girlfriend come and join us and we will try and pass the time away." We joined those young people and had an enjoyable time with music and songs.[16]

Besides the emphasis on traditional music, however, some performer-passengers on the radio program also played original and topical songs, many of which often seemed anomalous to the production. In the third and last series, therefore, one of the regular travellers became an accordionist and Conductor Jack took over most of the singing duties, performing Newfoundland favorites like "Squid Jigging Ground" and "Hard, Hard Times."

Another important area of aural conventions in "The Newfie Bullet" was the oral narrations and story-telling events which constituted significant variety segments for many shows, often being integrally linked with musical performances. Singing and story-telling sessions were especially prevalent at impromptu "times" which emerged at Christmas and New Years and on occasions of engine breakdown or stoppage. Thus, on one Christmas Eve Foley suggested "that we entertain ourselves as our forefathers have done for centuries. That we go around the circle and each of us got to sing or play something or tell a story or whatever."[17] The oral narratives of the series were well tailored to fit the scenes and plots of the dramas. The predominant genres were exemplary memorates, humorous anecdotes and explanatory historical accounts. Moreover, two programs that featured the narration of ghost stories aired railroad legends of actual oral currency in Newfoundland, "The Vanishing Brakeman" and the "Phantom Bullet," both of which exhibit well known international motifs.[18] It was the localization of the details of these legends, however, as well as the contexts, style and language of their performances which made them seem like real past events.

Folk speech permeated not only the oral narratives of the show but the dialogue throughout and was an indispensable ingredient in the communication of a familiar, old-time Newfoundland social atmosphere. Especially prominent in this vein were dialect usages (e.g., "that dirty sleeveen"; "he poisons me!") and proverbial phrases and comparisons (e.g., "it's all water under the stage now"; "like a sculpin in a school of herring"; "he's got his nose up every dog's hole, that one").

If the aural conventions of "The Newfie Bullet" guided the listening audience to Newfoundland's past then the conventionalized settings of the radio drama brought them to an outport home. The majority of the social interaction that took place on the program occurred in a passenger car of the train which can be likened to the "front room" of a traditional Newfoundland house, and in the caboose which functioned as a Newfoundland kitchen. Students of Newfoundland society and culture have shown that the "front room" of a Newfoundland household is a formal space where outsiders are entertained and where symbols of status and class assert themselves.[19] On the other hand, the Newfoundland kitchen is not only a space for food preparation and eating, but it is a place of egalitarian socializing and collective merry-making. As the radio show developed, it became clear that the caboose of the "Bullet" was a private, tea-drinking space which accommodated the egalitarian and sometimes intimate interactions of Conductor Jack Foley and two other main characters. In contrast, the passenger car was depicted as a public place which housed strangers of various nationalities, backgrounds, classes and interest groups who went through a great many conflicts and attempted resolutions. The plots may be interpreted in terms of these two spaces because the happy final resolution of many programs was that, functionally speaking, once the conflicts with strangers were reconciled the passenger car *became* the caboose, the new happy primary group making personal comments to one another, sharing food and drink, playing music, singing and in general having a real Newfoundland "time."

Another aspect of setting which directly lent itself to the nostalgic myth of "Old Newfoundland" was that the train itself was sometimes likened to a fishing vessel. For instance, one of the inebriated characters made this observation:

It's like I told ya, my father was a conductor on a train, but he was treated like a sea captain. Everybody called him skipper. See in Newfoundland, we didn't know anything about trains, but we knew everything there was to know about boats, so we treated the train like a vessel that sailed overland.[20]

More than just a vehicle associated with fishing, the railway itself was sometimes depicted as a Newfoundland way of life that was threatened with extinction by nefarious forces:

It used to be more than just a job working on the Railway, my God the men who built her . . . . My Father used to talk about the first war—they used to work day and night—and if anything broke down, a man would go to his own kitchen to find a bit of wire or whatever it took to fix her up, to hear him tell it most of the trains were held together with fishing line . . . and now, to think that there's talk of doing away with the railway, it's as if all this sacrifice meant nothing. Only a man with no heart at all would want to take away our railway. . . . [21]

The conventionalized characters which emerged in the final season of "The Newfie Bullet" were Conductor Jack Foley, Clara Squires, a middle aged spinster with a painful past, and Dan Picco, an intelligent but lazy, "hangashore" alcoholic. What they resembled as a group, however, was a happy, mutually supportive nuclear family. As a father-figure Jack Foley was a symbol of authority, order and justice (e.g., he chased Dan Picco off the train for gambling). He often fulfilled his merciful role as father in ways that betrayed his human frailty, however, sometimes to a point of absurdity (e.g., he had the train back up for miles in order to help a boy who was threatened with punishment if he did not find his shoe). Perhaps Jack's greatest failings were evident in his love-hate relationship with his dissolute son-figure, Dan Picco, with whom he often lost his temper. For his part, Picco usually behaved as a spoiled adolescent, unwilling to face manhood. Dan cared for and loved to please his parent-figures but he shirked as many responsibilities as possible, concentrating his energies on accordion-playing, drinking rum, free-loading, having great times and hustling his way through life on a train that he was clearly on for the ride.

A provider of physical comforts, especially tea, as well as a constant counsel to Jack, Clara was a pillar of family stability who as a mother-figure successfully maintained the peace between father and son with admonishments such as, "That's enough Dan!" and "Shame on you, Jack!"

Clearly these conventionalized characterizations did not necessarily lend themselves to nostalgia. The program's sitcom plots which focused on a happy confusion framed by a normality of love and laughter did, however, for the human problems that they dramatized were all based on simple errors that were handily remedied or explained through a straightforward adherence to old notions and tried truths. For example, one episode revolved around the confusion which began when Dan Picco answered an ad from the provincial Department of Tourism for a leader of guided tours.[22] Unfortunately Picco was allowed to think that what the Department wanted was for someone to deliver "gutted turrs" (sea bird). Much to the surprise of Conductor Foley, who knowingly let Picco commit his error and was admonished for it at the time, Dan got the job anyway and took a group of tourists on the train, thereby causing havoc for Foley. Since Picco did not know what to say to the tourists, he was advised by Foley to fabricate place-name legends for communities like Foxtrap, Hatchet Cove, Dildo and Piper's Hole. Dan then inveigled Jack to help him and after a few more misunderstandings the hassles that Jack brought upon himself were accidentally resolved and happiness reigned. For many, the nostalgic appeal of such a "problem-solving paradigm" from the past is that, as Horace Newcomb has observed, "there is a warmth that emerges from the corrected mistakes, a sort of ultimate human companionship."[23]

The conventions of characterization and plot that developed in the nostalgic sitcom formula of "The Newfie Bullet" are in fact quite standard and are evident in well-known programs like "Happy Days." However, the extensive use of folklore within the conventionalized systems of sound and setting in "The Newfie Bullet" gave the resulting nostalgia a mythic effect with a distinctly Newfoundland flavor.

In conclusion, it might be noted that the nostalgic experience is sometimes criticized as being overly fanciful, excessively escapist and potentially dangerous. Yet it can also be understood as an adaptive mechanism to allay anxieties in times of rapid cultural change. To partially paraphrase a metaphor employed by Fred Davis, the nostalgic experience is a conservative one which deposits past happiness in the bank of memory, thereby giving one a sense of current worth and a "claim on the future."[24] Some Newfoundland listeners may well have experienced CBC's "Newfie Bullet" in this manner.

Notes

[1]The Canadian Broadcasting Corporation (CBC) scripts and tapes of this program have been deposited by David Ross in the Memorial University of Newfoundland Folklore and Language Archive (MUNFLA), accession number 81-513. Scripts are located in PD 523, folders 1 through 40. My definition of nostalgia is partially based on the ideas contained in Fred Davis's stimulating essay, "Nostalgia, Identity and the Current Nostalgia Wave," *Journal of Popular Culture*, 11:2 (Fall,1977), 414-424.

[2]Two recent treatments of the Newfoundland Railway are Chapter 17, "The Politics and Economics of the Newfoundland Railway," in Frederick W. Rowe's *A History of Newfoundland and Labrador* (Toronto: McGraw-Hill Ryerson, 1980), pp. 327-339, and "The Railway in Newfoundland" issue of *Decks Awash*, 10:4 (August 1981).

[3]See the notes for the long-playing record by The Newfoundland Symphony Orchestra, *The Newfie Bullet—A Newfoundland Journey* (St. John's: Turnabout Canadiana Collection LTC-32010, 1981).

[4]Lester V. Berrey and Melvin Van den Bark, *The American Thesaurus of Slang: A Complete Reference Book of Colloquial Speech* (New York: Crowell, 1943) and G.M. Story, W.J. Kirwin, J.D.A. Widdowson, eds. *Dictionary of Newfoundland English* (Toronto: Univ. of Toronto Press, 1982). In addition see p. 58 of *Media Sense*.

[5]See "Newfie Jokes" by Gerald Thomas in Edith Fowke, *Folklore of Canada* (Toronto: McClelland and Stewart, 1976), pp. 142-153.

[6]Variants of these songs with explanatory notes may be found in two submissions of Neil Rosenberg ("Newfoundland"; "The *Newfoundland Express* Again") to the special features on Canadian railroad songs edited by Tim Rogers in the *Canadian Folk Music Bulletin*, 16:2/4 (April/October, 1982). For the "Wabash Cannonball" parodic cycle see my statement, " 'The Wabash Cannonball' Parodic Song Cycle," *Canadian Folk Music Bulletin*, 16:4 (October, 1982), 26.

[7]This particular verse was collected by Brendan White, MUNFLA accession number 78-96. White collected the song from his father who maintains that the song was written at the Gander base where he was stationed.

[8]Michael T. Wall, *More of Canada's Singing Newfoundlander* (Halifax: Banff SBC 5422, 1975).

[9]The Newfoundland Symphony Orchestra.

[10]Interview with David Ross, May 25, 1982, MUNFLA accession number 82-170, C5792.

[11]An example of this approach is Tom Burns, "Folklore in the Mass Media: Television," *Folklore Forum* 2:4 (1969), 90-106.

[12]John G. Cawelti, *The Six-Gun Mystique* (Bowling Green, Ohio: Bowling Green University Popular Press, 1970), p. 27.

[13]Marshall McLuhan, *Understanding Media: The Extensions of Man* (New York: McGraw-Hill, Signet Books, 1964), p. 263.

[14]These negative symbols are well documented in Leo Marx, *The Machine in the Garden* (New York: Oxford, 1967), pp. 145-226.

[15]MUNFLA, 81-513, PD 523, Folder No. 21, p. 20.

[16]Victor Butler, *The Little Nord Easter: Reminiscences of a Placentia Bayman*, Wilfred Wareham, editor (St. John's: Memorial University of Newfoundland, 1975), p. 102.

[17]MUNFLA, 81-513, PD 523, Folder No. 36, p. 11.

[18]MUNFLA, 81-513, PD 523, Folders No. 7 and 21; Ernest W. Baughman, *Type and Motif Index of the Folktales of England and North America* (The Hague: Mouton, 1966), Motifs: E599.7 (ghost carries lantern); E535.4 (phantom railway train).

[19]For the symbolic significance of hooked rugs in terms of these rooms see Gerald L. Pocius, "Hooked Rugs in Newfoundland: The Representation of Social Structure in Design," *Journal of American Folklore*, 92 (1979), 273-284.

[20]MUNFLA, 81-513, Folder No. 2, p. 15.

[21]*Ibid.*, Folder No. 15, pp. 28-29.

[22]*Ibid.*, Folder No. 18.

[23]Horace Newcomb, *TV: The Most Popular Art* (New York: Anchor Press, 1974), p. 41.

[24]Davis, 420.

Of Scoffs, Mounties and Mainlanders:
The Popularity of a Sheep-Stealing Ballad
in Newfoundland

Michael Taft

IN NEWFOUNDLAND, locally composed ballads sometimes become commercially successful popular songs. The transformation from local popularity to island-wide acclaim involves a number of interrelated and complex factors. An investigation of these factors reveals something of the role which traditional culture plays in influencing and shaping local popular culture, as well as the effects of popular culture on local traditions. The popular ballad "Aunt Martha's Sheep" has been the most commercially successful song composed in Newfoundland in recent years. The reasons for its popularity may shed some light on the interrelationships between folk and popular culture.[1]

On October 22, 1972, the Newfoundland radio station VOCM sponsored the "Newfoundland Gold Record Night," a gala event held at the St. John's Arts and Culture Centre. The affair was billed as "an historic occasion as Newfoundland and Newfoundlanders everywhere pay tribute to the musical ambassadors who have emblazoned our province on the world's entertainment map."[2] Several local performers were given public recognition for their contribution in the field of Newfoundland popular music, but the highlight of the evening, and indeed the primary reason for the event, was the awarding of a gold record to singer Dick Nolan for his recording of the song "Aunt Martha's Sheep." The presentation was made by the premier of the province, Frank Moores, and the occasion was topped off by Nolan's live performance of the song.

Dick Nolan is perhaps Newfoundland's most successful and prolific performer. He was born in 1939 in the west coast Newfoundland city of Corner Brook. He began his career in that city with a local country and western band, but by the late 1950s he had moved to Toronto, where he played and toured with mainland professional performers. He began making records in 1959 and has issued at least eighteen long playing albums.[3] At first, he was a Johnny Cash imitator who had only limited success in the Canadian popular market, but in 1966 he redirected his talents toward Newfoundland audiences by recording Newfoundland popular and traditional songs. He is now a very successful artist, and the song "Aunt Martha's Sheep" in many ways marks the high point of his professional career:[4]

Aunt Martha's Sheep

Come gather all around me and I'll sing to you a tale
About the boys in Carmenville who almost went to jail
It happened on a November's night when all hands was asleep
We crept up over Joe Tulk's hill and stole Aunt Martha's sheep.

Now, if you pay attention, I know I'll make you laugh
We never went to steal the sheep, we went to steal the calf
The old cow she got angry 'cause we woke her from her sleep
We couldn't take any chances, so we had to steal the sheep.

We caught the woolly animal and dragged her from her pen
She said good-bye to the little lambs she'd never see again
She knew that those dark strangers soon would take her life
In less than half an hour she felt the dreadful knife.

Aunt Martha she got angry when she heard about the loss
She said she'd catch the robbers, no matter what the cost
Next morning just as [sic] sunrise she to the office went
And to the RCMP a telegram she sent.

The Mountie got the message and started in to read
This is from Aunt Martha telling an awful deed
Last night my sheep was stolen by whom I cannot tell
I'd like for you to catch them and to drag them back to jail.

Just a short time later about twelve o'clock that night
We had the sheep a-cooking and everyone feeling tight
The smell of mutton and onions no man could ask for more
We were chug-luggin' Dominion when a Mountie walked in the door.

Said, "Sorry boys, your party I really don't want to wreck
I smelled the meat a-cooking and I had to come in and check
You see, the sheep was stolen and the thief is on the loose"
I said, "Come right in and join us sir, we're having a piece of moose."

He said, "Thanks a lot" and he sat right down, and I gave him a piece of the sheep
"This is the finest piece of moose I know I've ever eat"
About two o'clock in the morning he bid us all good-day
"If we get any clues on the sheep, sir, we'll phone you right away.

He said, "Thanks a lot, you're a darn fine bunch, and your promise I know you'll
    keep
And if everyone was as good as you, she wouldn't have lost her sheep."
After he left we had the piece we had in the oven to roast
We might have stole the sheep, boys, but the Mountie ate the most.[5]

This song is typical of Newfoundland popular music in that its theme
and lyrical structure closely resemble local traditional ballads. The "come-
all-ye" beginning, the use of the local place names and personalities, as
well as the rhyme scheme and stanza structure, are all reminiscent of
traditional Newfoundland balladry. Compare the first stanza of "Aunt
Martha's Sheep" with that of the traditional Newfoundland ballad "The
Wreck of the Steamship *Florizel*":

Attention, fellow countrymen, while this sad tale I'll tell
About the well-known steamboat, the S.S. *Florizel*
Who gravely harmed up near Renews, the steamer came to grief;
Caught in a blinding snowstorm, she ran upon a reef.[6]

The recording of "Aunt Martha's Sheep" features an accompanying
button accordion, which is one of the traditional musical instruments on
the island; but, unlike traditional Newfoundland ballads, its rhythm is
upbeat and Nolan's singing is also accompanied by drums and an electric
guitar.

The question which arises with most pieces of Newfoundland
popular music is whether there is a traditional source for the song. Is the
song an entirely innovative creation or has the songwriter consciously
adapted an older, locally-composed ballad? In the case of "Aunt Martha's

Sheep," although the copyright credits are to Nolan and Ellis Coles, there is evidence to suggest that the song was adapted from a ballad written thirty years earlier.

In 1942 a man named Arthur Butt was hospitalized for several months. The people of his community would visit him and tell him the news of the day. Once they told him of two boys who had stolen a sheep from an old woman in the community. The boys were apprehended by the law, tried and convicted. Since Butt had nothing to do but "count the knotholes in the ceiling,"[7] he decided to make up a song about the incident, which he called "Aunt Allie's Sheep":

Come all ye boys of Newfoundland
and listen to my tale,
It's about two boys from Perry's Cove who got lately put in jail.
It happened on one Sunday night when all were fast asleep
They went up over Bull-Birds-Hill
and they stole Aunt Allie's sheep.

Now to continue with my song
I'm sure 'twill make you laugh,
They didn't mean to take the sheep
They meant to steal the calf.
But they made the old cow angry
When they woke her from her sleep,
And Mike said, "Hal, we'll run no risk
We'll have to take the sheep."

They took the woolly animal
And dragged her from her pen,
She bid good-bye to her dear young lambs
Which she never would see again.
For she knew these brave young heros
Would take away her life,
And within half an hour
She felt that fatal knife.

Mike Power grew suspicious
When he learned of his sad loss,
He meant to find the robber
No matter what the cost.
He notified the policemen
Who were quickly on the scene,
But no clue of the stolen animal
Could anywhere be seen.

But he didn't lose his courage
For he knew he was in luck,

He saw something very "sheepish"
About the boy called Mike.
He asked the boys some questions
Whick [sic] they refused to tell,
But when he turned to windward
He smelled the nicest smell.

The fleece was in the cellar
But he found the meat upstairs,
And when he searced [sic] the oven
Their eyes filled up with tears.
He took the meat out in his hand
Although it was steaming hot,
But what surprised them most of all
He never took the pot!

Well, Ann began to criticize
And Hal began to wail,
But Mike said he was doggoned
If they'd lock him up in jail.
But the policemen grabbed him by the coat
And locked them in the car,
And within half an hour
They were up before the bar.

The Judge, he looked them over
And I'm sure he lost no time,
He asked if they were ever there
For any other crime.
And Mike he looked up into his face
With a voice so loud and clear,
"I was here one time your honour,
For stealing Martha's beer."

The Judge then passed their sentence
Which seemed so awful cheap,
It was only thirty days in jail
And twelve dollars for the sheep.
"But if you do the like again
I want to make it clear;
Instead of thirty days in jail
I'll give you both a year."[8]

A comparison will clearly show that the first three and a half stanzas of Nolan's song are substantially the same as Arthur Butt's song.

Nolan says that he heard a local performer from Marystown, Newfoundland sing "Aunt Martha's Sheep" several years before he decided to record the song, and that, at that time, the song was attributed to Ellis Coles, a song-writer in Carmenville, Newfoundland. After some correspondence between the two men, Nolan received the lyrics of the song from Coles. It is difficult to determine how Coles gained access to Butt's song (two hundred miles separate their home communities), but it is possible to make some educated guesses.

Butt's song was quite popular in Perry's Cove, as well as in the surrounding area. In his words,

it was a household thing; we all sang it at one time or another, at our Christmas concerts—you know, everybody knew about it. . . . Everybody in Perry's Cove knew the song and the people outside Perry's Cove . . . . I sang it myself in the Orange Hall. I sang it around to different people's houses, when we were celebrating at Christmas, you know.

In addition to its wide oral circulation, Butt's brother wrote out the song for people who requested copies, and in more recent times, Butt has photocopied the song and given it to friends and to the customers of his auto body repair business.

Many of the inhabitants of Perry's Cove, like Arthur Butt himself, moved to larger urban areas,[9] and have undoubtedly spread the song further. Whether Coles heard the song from a Perry's Cove resident, obtained one of the handwritten or xeroxed broadsides, or discovered the song in a more indirect manner is not known, but the point is that over the last thirty years the song "Aunt Allie's Sheep" has been fairly accessible on the island.

The source of the tune to "Aunt Martha's Sheep" is a bit more difficult to determine. Nolan adapted the tune used by the Marystown singer. Butt would not sing his version of the song, since he felt that his voice could not compete with Nolan's ("nobody can sing as well as Dick Nolan"). He did say that almost any tune could be put to his song and that it was sung to "just a bit of ordinary old music." Residents of the Perry's Cove area, however, claim that the tune of "Aunt Allies Sheep" is the same as that of "Aunt Martha's Sheep," but slower in tempo.[10]

As in other Anglo-American song traditions, Newfoundlanders tend to create lyrics but borrow tunes. This is certainly the case with the Butt-Nolan songs. Parts of the tune are similar to the tune family which includes "Son of a Gun," "Son of a Gambolier," "Dunderbeck" and "Rambling Wreck from Georgia Tech," as well as to the more recent song "Sink the Bismarck."[11] All of these songs, however, vary considerably from the Butt-Nolan songs in their overall tune structures. Perhaps a closer tune analogue is "The Foot of the Mountain Brow" (Laws P7), which is a familiar song in the folk and popular repertoires of Newfoundland singers.[12] The tune to "Aunt Martha's Sheep" may well be an unconscious composite of these various songs.

Whatever the source, the tune is certainly a familiar-sounding type of melody to the Newfoundland ear. Nolan's accordion accompanist, Wilf Doyle, said that he simply improvised in the recording studio without previous rehearsal, which indicates the familiar nature of the tune.[13]

Whether the song and its tune are "traditional" or not, the story it tells is certainly an old and familiar one. It has similarities to both Aarne-Thompson type 1525M, *Mak and the Sheep*, and 1525H*, *The Theft of a Sheep*, under the general type 1525, *The Master Thief*.[14] Stories of clever stealing or poaching of food are common, not only in Newfoundland but in the entire Atlantic region of Canada. The following two stories, one from Newfoundland and the other from Nova Scotia, both have many similarities to the story of "Aunt Martha's Sheep":

My father always told the story of my Uncle Art, and how he fooled the RCMP. My uncle was in the country, moose-hunting, and he was staying in a "camp." At night a group of hunters would gather at the camp for drinking and telling stories. The RCMP officer came to the camp one night. He had just caught someone poaching, and had the [moose] heart for evidence. The mountie was invited to pull up a chair and have a beer, which he did, putting the heart down by the chair. By and by, the mountie was beginning to feel the effects of the beer. My uncle, on one of his trips to the kitchen for more beer, managed to sneak the heart into the kitchen. He cut it up in pieces, fried it, and brought it out to the men, all of whom, including the mountie, soon made short work of the moose's heart, the evidence. Not a word was said about the man's poaching.[15]

Reminiscent of the caption "Children do say the darndest things" is the story told by a young woman of a sister when young, in this regard. When moose were much more plentiful than at the present time, some person might in the closed season, kill a bull moose, not for sport, but as an addition to the supply of meat for his family. A young farmer with a young family had done so, and warned his children not to mention moose meat before a visitor to the home.

The game warden, happening to stop at the man's home, one day, being a relative and a friend of the family was invited to stay to dinner. Moose meat may not have been served, but the little girl, evidently wishing to obey her father, and perhaps to impress the visitor, at the dinner table held up a piece of meat upon her fork and remarked, "Look Uncle John, papa killed the old sow."[16]

Similarly, the themes of stealing livestock and poaching had been popular with Newfoundland composers and singers long before "Aunt Martha's Sheep." In the late nineteenth century, three men were caught poaching trout by a constable named Bishop, and were sentenced to terms in jail. A local priest was sympathetic to the poachers and composed a poem on the subject which was issued in a community newspaper. The title of the poem is "Vindicator" and the only lines which are extant are "When those two boys, were living on Switchel and Dry/Bishop was having an Elegant fry."[17]

Some time in the early part of this century, the well-known satirical song-writer and broadside balladeer, Johnny Burke of St. John's, composed a song entitled "The Widow's Goat":

> Oh, last Sunday night at 12 o'clock,
>   Three city sports put on their coats,
> And heeled it for the Battery Road,
>   To capture Widow Dooley's goats.
> When they arrived upon the scene,
>   But soon accosted by a man,
> But Darby Davis didn't mind—
>   He put his flash-light on the nan.
>
> Ho, oh, bad cess to Darby Davis,
>   We'll put a bullet in his head,
> When next he's seen on the Battery Road,
>   To capture goats when we're in bed.
> We'll get a lead on Monkey Face,
>   Call Davis himself a man,
> To come around when graveyards yawn
>   To capture a lone widow's nan.
>
> Oh, with lamps and ropes and walking sticks,
>   And elevated slights from booze,
> They soon arrived on Battery Road
>   And round their necks soon had a noose.
> Then quickly hastened from the scene
>   As up the road they did retreat,
> Till they were captured on the Cross
>   By two policemen on their beat.
>
> In single file they marched away
>   Till they arrived at Flower Hill,
> When Widow Dooley's stately goats
>   These bold assassins soon did kill.
> Each put a quarter on his hump,
>   And soon was frying on a pan,
> When half a dozen hungry mouths,
>   Demolished Widow Dooley's nan.
>
> Now women watch the Block House well,
>   With brooms and pickets get in shape,
> And keep your gig lamps on the Block

When Darby Davis rounds the Cape.
For mind you do, if not you'll rue,
  Nail up your doors in each abode,
For Davis, he won't leave a kid,
  Or damn the goat, on Battery Road.

Now women mind your nanny goats
  And lash them tightly in the shop,
And watch for Davis on his rounds,
  When watering for a mutton chop,
Your opera glasses brighten up,
  Look out for Davis, Doyle and Flynn,
If they don't catch them on the ground
  They're sure to take your goats to wing.[18]

Burke also wrote a song entitled "Betsey Brennan's Blue Hen," in which he uses the stealing theme as a vehicle for several instances of humorous cursing:[19]

From the widow McKenny
I bought for a penny,
To lay a few eggs
  When the berries are ripe;
But some dirty crawler
From the hen house did haul her,
  My beautiful little blue hen he did swipe.

May his whisker turn green
When he eats crubeen,
And may pork fat and beans
  Nearly make him insane;
May two dogs and a crackie
Eat all his tobaccie,
  The villain who stole my little Blue Hen.

Oh, this hen she had dozens
Of nephews and cousins,
The world round
  I would roam for her sake;
But some wicked savage
To grease his white cabbage.
Walked off with my hen and my beautiful drake.

May her stockings fall down
When she goes out of town;
May her hair on her crown,
  She can't bob it, and then;
May the girls from the Nor'ard,

Stick pins in her forehead,
   The villain who lifted my little Blue Hen.

I bought from Port Saunders
That hen and two ganders,
But some dirty clown
   From my hen house did steal;
My beautiful chicken,
I would have for pickin'
On Christmas Day
   To have a fine meal.

May the ravenous baste
Burst her blouse in the waist;
May she not get a taste
   Of a dumplin' or cake;
May the man from Freshwater
Go back on her daughter,
   That lifted my hen and my beautiful drake.

I would search the seas over
From Boston to Dover,
To find out the rover,
   And wouldn't stop then;
I would walk to Trepassey
To collar the lassie,
   Who pilfered my dear little beautiful hen.

May the measels and gout,
When he chance to go out
On his double chain mouth
   Shove him down in the Pen;
By the curse of Belloram,
May he never stop roar'n
   The villain who lifted my little Blue Hen.

May his pipe never smoke;
May his tea pot be broke,
And to add to the joke
   May his kettle not boil;
May he bust on could tay
When he drinks any day,
   And his ton of foxey whiskers may soon go to oil.

May his clothes be in rags,
And his trousers bread bags;
May he stagger from jags
   If he goes round the lake;

And may he have bunions,
As big as small onions,
   The scoundrel who lifted my beautiful drake.[20]

A variant of this song, "Betsy's Cock," has become well established in the repertoires of a number of traditional singers and has been collected several times. The addition of a sexual double-entendre increases the humor of the song:

Attention all both great and small,
Come listen onto me.
When I relate a tale of daring rob-bery.
T'was on a dark September night,
The dew lay on each rock,
When two young men made up their minds,
To try to steal a cock.

They started off on that same night,
The rooster for to take.
They made such noise in capturing him,
Poor Betsy they did wake.
She got up and dressed herself,
It didn't take her long.
And then she said to Alice May,
My lovely cock is gone.

She started for the harbour,
The dark and stormy night.
And swore by all she would go in
Wherever she saw a light.
They held a dance on that same night,
It was nearing twelve o'clock,
When Betsy jumped out on the floor,
Crying "someone stole my cock."
But if he's in the house tonight,
I pray him pay me here,
But none offered her the cash,
The rooster wasn't there.

She wished the man that stole him,
Would meet a watery grave,
And the boat that he was cook on,
Would sink beneath the waves.
But her wishes were not granted,
And Betsy did forget,
She owes me a gallon of berries,
She never paid me yet.

Now to conclude and finish,
I hope you will agree,
And never go cock stealing,
Above the sparrow tree.
And remember the dark September night,
They stole poor Betsy's dick,
Don't go to a lonely widow's house,
And play her a dirty trick.[21]

In 1960, Kenneth Peacock collected the ballad "The Moose Song" from its author, George Croucher. As in the poem "Vindicator," the poacher is a sympathetic figure; a moose happens to wander into a community and is promptly killed and butchered, even though this is against the game-laws. The moose meat is shared among the members of the community, but an informer in the crowd runs to the law. The judge is sympathetic to the poachers and gives them only a nominal fine. The song ends with a threat to the informer: "And now my song is ending I'm going to propose/It's going to pay the squealer b'y to keep his big mouth closed."[22] This song has since been recorded by two Newfoundland professional performers, Wilf Doyle, the accordionist on Nolan's song, and Edison Williams.[23] It is unlikely that either performer knew the Peacock version, but rather they acquired the song from oral sources.

The fact, however, that Nolan's "Aunt Martha's Sheep" has substantial traditional roots in Newfoundland culture does not entirely explain its widespread popularity. The analogues to Nolan's song given above have been at best only moderately popular on the island. The priest's "vindication" of the poachers survives only as a fragment and did not enter tradition. Burke's "The Widow's Goat," unlike some of his other songs, has not become part of the repertoire of Newfoundland singers. "Betsey Brennan's Blue Hen" did enter oral tradition some fifty years ago, when George Allan England reported that it was the favorite song of the sealers on the ship *Terra Nova*,[24] but it has not been collected since that time. "Betsy's Cock" is still quite popular in one area of the island, and is often sung in conjunction with "Christy's Dick"—an equally risque song about the accidental loss of a chicken—but the song has not gained island-wide acceptance.

Perhaps the most popular of the "Aunt Martha's Sheep" analogues has been "The Moose Song" which has been recorded twice, but even this song has not become a Newfoundland "hit" in the way that Nolan's song has. "Aunt Martha's Sheep" has sold over 100,000 copies in Canada, most being bought by the people on the island or by expatriate Newfoundlanders in the mainland centres of Halifax, Montreal and Toronto. In addition, the song has had more air-time on local radio stations than probably any other locally composed song.

Part of the reason for the song's popularity is that Dick Nolan is one of Newfoundland's most popular artists. He has discovered the right blend of Newfoundland material and country and western style to make his performances extremely appealing to island audiences. For this reason alone, any song that Nolan sings has a better than average chance of becoming a bestseller. Another factor in the song's popularity may be that "Aunt Martha's Sheep" marks the beginning of Nolan's contract with RCA Records. Previously, he had recorded for Arc Records, a small independent company that had neither the money nor the incentive to publicize Nolan's talents. RCA has been quite active in keeping the Newfoundland public aware of their recording artists.

These factors, however, do not really explain why the specific song "Aunt Martha's Sheep" has been so successful. Nolan has sung many songs, and none of them has been a popular as "Aunt Martha's Sheep." We must look at the song itself in order to determine the reasons for its success in the Newfoundland market and its ultimate incorporation into the traditional repertoire of the island culture.

Nolan's song combines three subjects which are traditional narrative themes in Newfoundland: the stolen feast, anti-authoritarianism, and the outsider or mainlander as dupe. There are countless anecdotes and memorates concerning the stealing of food for a clandestine feast. This is generally called a "scoff" in Newfoundland dialects,[25] and this pranking custom often happens on special occasions.[26] The following account occurs during a wake:

About 3 a.m. Leo came up with the idea of cooking a scoff. So without giving it any thought Mark and I said: "That's a fine idea: we'll go out to Aunt Polly's garden and get (steal) the vegetables; she's got a fine stock." We fetched a bag and three of us went out leaving Uncle Tim behind to keep the "fire in."

About half an hour later we arrived back with a head of cabbage, some potatoes, carrots and a large turnip, only to find that Uncle Tim was sound asleep on the couch by the stove. Luckily, the corpse was all right; no cat had come into the room.[27]

The scoff was often performed on such holidays as Halloween, April Fool's Day, or Bonfire Night, along with other pranks and practical jokes, but a stolen feast was also the type of prank which was not limited to any special time. A scoff might occur whenever there was food for the taking:

When we were boys, one thing we used to do in the fall of the year was what we called *scoffing*. In the fall, people's vegetables were starting to be big enough to eat. Often, a gang of boys would get together, and steal so much vegetables, and a chicken or something from someone and cook it.

Some of the boys would get destructive about it. We'd go along by a fence of a garden, reach through and get the vegetables. Some would pull up say carrots, and if they weren't big enough, would poke them back down in the ground again.

I can remember one fellow who would take his mother's chickens for his scoffing. The next day, when she discovered them gone, she'd send him all over the harbour, looking for these chickens, that he'd eaten the night before.[28]

It seems that boys were boys in those days and grandfather was no exception. One year on the way back from Labrador with a full load of fish, the skipper thought the wind would freshen too much during the night and he decided to harbour for the evening. It seems that quite a few other skippers decided to make for the same front.

During the night most everybody went ashore, and while wandering around the harbour, grandfather spotted a beautiful bush of ripe currants in a garden and the temptation was too great. On his way back to the schooner later that night he cut a hole in the wooden fence and broke the bush off close to the ground and took it on board. After feasting on the currants he tossed the bush overboard for the tide to carry away the evidence.

The next morning there was an awful uproar. The men of the harbour searched high and low, ashore and afloat, trying to get a clue as to who stole the clergyman's prize currant bush.[29]

Richard S. Tallman has pointed out that pranks exist in narrative form as much as in play activity,[30] and this is certainly true of the scoff-prank. There is almost as much delight in telling of a scoff as in participating in one. "Aunt Martha's Sheep" tells of thieves who are engaged in just such a scoff, although perhaps on a slightly grander scale than was usual. Fruits, vegetables and the odd chicken were more commonly taken, but pigs, goats, calves and sheep were also scoffed, as we have seen from the accounts of Johnny Burke and Arthur Butt.

It is important to note that the scoff-prank is not considered a serious crime in Newfoundland culture, but as Faris has said, "[It] is sanctioned within limits " (p. 162). The food stolen must be for one's own feast. Stealing food for re-sale, or for personal profit of any sort, is not a scoff and is not tolerated by the community. The following newspaper account is serious in tone, indicating that a non-sanctioned crime has been committed:

HOLYROOD—Three Kelligrews men, all in their early 20s, have been charged in connection with the theft Tuesday of a truck load of vegetables from an Upper Gullies farmer.

An RCMP spokesman said two of the defendants were arrested in Bay de Verde where they were in the process of selling the stolen goods. The other was arrested in Kelligrews.

The vegetables were stolen from James Coates, who owns a farm on Andrew's Road in Upper Gullies. Most of the vegetables have been recovered.

The spokesman said Mr. Coates is now in the process of assessing the damage to his property which he termed "considerable."

He said the thieves did more damage to the farm than just stealing the vegetables. "For every head of cabbage they stole they damaged two."
The three defendants will appear before the magistrate Saturday.[31]

Although the thieves in this case stole the vegetables and committed vandalism in much the same manner as scoffers might, their intent in stealing the food was quite different, and consequently they overstepped the limits of tacit approval for such crimes in the community.

They further overstepped the limits in that the vegetables stolen were the livelihood of the victim. Food taken in a scoff-prank must not mean the loss of income for the grower; private gardens or non-commercial livestock are fair game for the pranksters. Consequently, there are no prank narratives concerning the stealing of fish left out to dry. Such an activity would be considered highly antisocial, since fishing is the livelihood of many Newfoundland communities.

The difference between a sanctioned and non-sanctioned extra-legal activity can be seen quite clearly in the tone of the following newspaper account. Note that knowledge of "Aunt Martha's Sheep" is assumed in the article:

It wasn't Aunt Martha's Sheep this time .... It was the real thing!
Mounties can tell the difference between moose and mutton, as two young men found out on Saturday.
While making a routine check of a car in the Bay Bulls area, what was reported to be a carcass of a moose calf was found in the trunk of a car.
The pair reportedly didn't have a moose or sheep hunting licence since there are no wild sheep in Newfoundland.
The meat is now in the custory [sic] of wildlife officials and the two are expected to be charged under the Wildlife Act.[32]

This is not a serious offense, but rather a humorous incident, as the allusion to Nolan's song indicates.

The reaction of the victim to the scoff must also be in accord with the community's perception of the crime. Attempting to find out who the wrongdoers were and turning them over to the authorities are sanctioned reprisals within the community. An overreaction by the victim would be as taboo as a scoffer overstepping the limits of the prank. The tone of shock is a bit exaggerated in the following article, but justified nevertheless in the eyes of Newfoundlanders:

DEER LAKE (Staff)—The boy heard the roar of the gun.
"He got me. I'm shot!," he cried.
You're at the movies, right?—The Cross and the Switchblade. Wrong.
Television then—Police Story? Wrong again.

A 16-year-old shot, stealing apples in a town in Canada's Happy Province? Right, believe it or not.[33]

"Aunt Martha's Sheep" is humorous and appealing to Newfoundlanders because it is a scoff-prank which falls well within the limits placed on sanctioned extra-legal activities. Both thieves and victim act the role expected of them in such a situation.

Anti-authoritarianism is also a common theme in Newfoundland folk narratives, and goes hand-in-hand with scoff stories. Often, as in the case of the stolen currant bush, the victim of the scoff-prank is an authority figure. There is a long tradition of jokes in Newfoundland which show disrespect for such important community figures as clergymen, teachers, doctors, politicians, judges and policemen.

But although these symbols of authority are laughed at, they are at the same time respected and feared, and are often used as threatening figures to misbehaving children.[34] The Royal Canadian Mounted Police, commonly called the RCMP or the Mounties, are perhaps the most visible symbol of authority in Newfoundland. They fulfill the role of provincial police and are the representatives of law and order in the outports and towns of the island. They are a constant threat to anyone engaged in illegal activities, sanctioned or non-sanctioned:

We used to steal sometimes too. Turnips and carrots were our specialty. I remember once that two boys and myself stole over a sack of turnips. We had to steal these things while they were in the ground. Several times the RCMP was called, but no one could find out who did it. When I was about 11 or 12 almost every day while the vegetables were in the ground you would hear of someone having some stolen.[35]

Often a verbal threat to call the RCMP would be used against the scoffers without the police actually being notified:

Another favourite thing we liked to do was to raid apple trees. We usually went in a small group to a house where we saw an apple tree. Usually some of the fellows would climb up in the tree and throw down the apples. Sometimes there would be someone on watch to make sure that we wouldn't get caught. We always managed to escape but the person who saw us running would often say "I know who you are and I'm going to call the mounties."[36]

It is doubtful that this threat prevented further scoffs, but rather it was intended to remind the wrong-doers of their extra-legal status in the community and to reinforce the authoritarian symbol of the RCMP. The threat is almost an essential ingredient of the pranking custom, whether it is verbalized or not.

Even in the generally approved activity of home-brewing, the threat might be implied, although not with the same seriousness as in the case of scoffing:

[For an April Fool's joke] perhaps a small plastic figure, say of a mountie, might be sent [to the victim] if it were known that the person made homebrew beer.[37]

Humor at the expense of the RCMP counteracts their threatening and authoritarian role and helps to relieve this point of tension in the community. In "Aunt Martha's Sheep" the threatening authority figure is turned into a fool who is made to believe that a sheep is a moose. In fact, the mountie in the song is doubly a fool, since not only does he not recognize a sheep when it is served to him, but he is tricked into becoming an accomplice to the thieves: "We might have stole the sheep, boys, but the Mountie ate the most." The song cleverly neutralizes the threatening authority of the RCMP officer, and thus is highly appealing to the Newfoundland audience.[38]

The third theme in Nolan's song, the outsider or mainlander as dupe, is not easily recognized unless one is aware that most RCMP officers are strangers to the community they serve; most, in fact, being from mainland Canada. Humor at the expense of the mainlander is most often expressed in Newfie Jokes, of which there are two major categories. By far the larger category portrays the Newfoundlander as stupid or dirty in exactly the same way as Polack Jokes describe Poles; but in the second category of Newfie Jokes, the Newfoundlander is portrayed as a clever trickster and the mainlander is the dupe, as in this example:

One day this mainlander was out cod jigging for sport in Conception Bay. While he was out there he met an old fisherman and inquired, "What are you catching?" The fisherman replied, "Newfoundland cod." The mainlander thinking he was going to get one over on the old fisherman asked, "How do you know it's Newfoundland cod and not Canadian cod?" "Well," says the Newfoundlander, "the ones with the big mouth we always throw back."[39]

The joke may simply assert the Newfoundlander's superiority over the mainlander, as in this two-liner:

Did you hear the one about the 16 Newfoundlanders who lived in an outhouse? They rented the basement apartment to twenty-four Torontonians.[40]

It is clear to any Newfoundlander who hears "Aunt Martha's Sheep" that a mainlander is being tricked by a native of the island. Only a mainlander would be so stupid as to mistake sheep for moose. The song is, among other things, an elaborate Newfie Joke.

The combination of these three themes, the stolen feast, anti-authoritarianism and the mainlander as dupe, explains the extreme popularity of "Aunt Martha's Sheep." None of the other stealing or poaching songs combines these themes, and consequently none are so popular. Johnny Burke's "The Widow's Goat" tells only of a scoff, and makes only passing reference to the police. The thieves are not portrayed as being particularly clever, and indeed the song seems to ridicule victim and scoffers alike in its overtly dramatic and hyperbolic style. In "Betsey Brennan's Blue Hen" and "Betsy's Cock" the scoff-theme is incidental to the devices of humorous cursing and double-entrendre.

Arthur Butt's "Aunt Allie's Sheep" displays no anti-authoritarianism, nor is a mainlander duped. The fact that the thieves are caught and punished makes the song a cautionary or moral tale rather than a truly humorous piece. "The Moose Song" is mildly anti-authoritarian, in that the judge is sympathetic to the poachers, but still the criminals are punished and there is no humor at the expense of outsiders. Only "Aunt Martha's Sheep" combines these three highly appealing themes in the proper proportion and only this ballad has obtained overwhelming success in the Newfoundland popular music market.

Three indications of the popularity of Nolan's song are that it has been recorded a number of times, it has generated two sequels, and at least two songs on a similar theme have also been recorded since 1972. Two Newfoundland performers, George Grandy and Albert Dean, have recorded "Aunt Martha's Sheep" as has New Brunswick singer Ben Weatherby.[41]

Dick Nolan has recorded a sequel to "Aunt Martha's Sheep" entitled "Courtroom in the Sky,"[42] in which he dreams that the case has come to court in heaven, with the mountie, Aunt Martha, the cow and finally the sheep all giving evidence. Ben Weatherby has also produced a sequel, "You Can't Fool a Newfoundlander,"[43] which plays on the mainlander-as-dupe theme. In this song, the mountie only pretends to be fooled, and comes back later, Aunt Martha in tow, to arrest the thieves. It turns out that the RCMP officer was not a mainlander, but a native of the island, which explains his craftiness.

These sequels have not attained the same degree of popularity as the original. Perhaps this is the nature of sequels in general, but no doubt their moralizing theme of "crime does not pay" has something to do with their lack of success.

George Grandy has recorded a song entitled "Aunt Lucy's Sheep"[44] which is to the same tune as Nolan's song, but is closer to Butt's ballad in that the sheep-stealers are apprehended and punished. Again, its lack of popularity probably lies in its moralizing theme. Given the nature of the crime as a sanctioned extra-legal activity, and the general sympathy for poachers and pranksters in Newfoundland culture, any song which shows justice prevailing in such a case would not be very popular.

Another Newfoundland singer, Ray McLean, has recorded a song entitled "The Mountie and the Moonshine,"[45] which like Nolan's song, is about common illegal activity on the island. A local inhabitant of a community promises to tell the RCMP who makes the moonshine in the area. The informer's secret testimony is this: "The man who makes the moonshine here makes the sunshine too." Thus the mountie is duped. The song shares many of the same thematic qualities with "Aunt Martha's Sheep" but perhaps improper promotion, the tune, or its slightly blasphemous nature account for its relative lack of popularity.

A further outgrowth of the popularity of "Aunt Martha's Sheep" is that it has been incorporated into local song and performance traditions on the island. The song is now quite commonly heard at informal "times"— the Newfoundland house party—and seems destined to become a traditional Newfoundland song.[46] I. Sheldon Posen has reported that the song is now a part of the repertoire of summer camp singers on the island,[47] which means that the ballad has gained acceptance with the young Newfoundland performer as well as the old. The newspaper article quoted above, entitled "The Real Thing!" suggests that the ballad's narrative has become a recognized dite on the island.

Perhaps the most interesting result of the incorporation of the song into local performance has been dramatic presentations of the song. Turning a popular song into a skit or play is not without precedent in Newfoundland. Arthur Scammell, composer of the highly popular Newfoundland song "Squid Jiggin' Ground," recalls that his song was acted out in school plays and talent shows.[48]

"Aunt Martha's Sheep" has been treated in this manner on at least two occasions. The present-day satirical song-writer Tom Cahill of St. John's wrote a play entitled "Aunt Martha's Sheep: A Comedy in One Act,"[49] which was performed in the St. John's area. The play is a courtroom comedy involving the crime of sheep-stealing and, according to Cahill, is based "on a fifteenth century French comedy of unknown authorship called 'La Farce de Maitre Patelin'." This is, of course, Aarne-Thompson type 1525 *The Lawyer's Mad Client*, but Cahill's immediate source for the play is, no doubt, much closer to home.

The play appears in a school reader under the title "Rory Aforesaid" and is credited to John Brandane,[50] although the editors also recognize that it is an adaptation of the French farce. The reader has been widely used in Newfoundland schools for several decades and thus the play is well-known to people on the island. The combining of a traditional tale, a popular school play and a popular ballad into a new dramatic work represents a blend of folk, literary and popular culture which is truly fascinating.

More recently a school in Carbonear put on a talent show in which the play "A Piece of Mutton" was performed.[51] The plot of this play is not known by this writer, but it also involves a courtroom comedy based on "Aunt Martha's Sheep." This may well be Cahill's play under a different title. It is interesting that Carbonear is the major town in the Perry's Cove area, where the ballad had its origin.

The ballad "Aunt Martha's Sheep" has come full circle, from traditional origins to island-wide popularity and then back into local performance situations. Its successful emergence and ultimate incorporation into the folk culture of Newfoundland is a result of its rather ingenious blend of musical styles and narrative themes. "Aunt Martha's Sheep" is truly a fine example of the interaction of folk and popular culture in Newfoundland.

Notes

[1] I should like to thank Charles Burke, Arthur Butt, Laurel Douchette, Martin Lovelace, Paul Mercer, Dick Nolan, John Scott, Wilfred Wareham, and the Memorial University of Newfoundland Folklore and Language Archive (hereafter MUNFLA) for their assistance with this paper. Permission to use material from MUNFLA was granted by the Director. I also wish to express my thanks to the following MUNFLA contributors upon whose information I have drawn: Eileen Beresford, Warrick J. Canning, Bobbie Fillier, Herbert Halpert, Mary E. Maynard, Hilda Murray, John Parsons, Edward E. Peddle, I. Sheldon Posen, Andrea Spurrell and John D. Widdowson.

[2] Newfoundland Gold Record Night souvenir program.

[3] For a discography of Nolan's recordings, see Michael Taft, *A Regional Discography of Newfoundland and Labrador, 1904-1972*, Bibliographic and Special Series, No. 1 (St. John's: MUNFLA, 1975), pp. 29-35.

[4] Most information on Dick Nolan is from a taped interview with him conducted by I. Sheldon Posen in St. John's, Newfoundland, 13 June 1972, MUNFLA 73-45/C1399-1401, and a telephone interview conducted by Michael Taft from Outer Cove, Newfoundland, 6 May 1976.

[5] Words and music by Dick Nolan and Ellis Coles, copyright c. 1972 Dunbar Music Canada Ltd. The words are reprinted from *The Ninth Edition of Newfoundland Songs* (St. John's: Bennett Brewing Co. Ltd., 1974), pp. 38-39, with permisskon od the authmp. I should likehank Gordon Cox for the muqkcal vrcnscription. This has been issued on *Fisherman's "my*, 12 inch 13rpm phonodiqc, RCA AAS-2574 John's, 1;72).

[6] Elisabeth E. Greenleaf and Grace Y. Mansfield, *Ballads and Sea Songs of Newfoundland* (1933; rpt. Hatboro, Penn.: Folklore Associates, 1968), p. 283.

[7] Most information on Butt and his song is from a taped intereview with him conducted by Michael Taft in St. John's, 22 Sept. 1975, MUNFLA 76-197.

[8] The lyrics of this song have been reprinted from the *Kesley United Church Journal (St. John's)*, 9 (Feb. 1973), p. 9, with permission of the author.

[9] Butt now lives in St. John's.

[10] I questioned students in an extension folklore course given in Carbonear by Wilfred Wareham, 8 Oct. 1975. Carbonear is only a few miles from Perry's Cove and many of the students were natives of the Perry's Cove area.

[11]I am indebted to Neil V. Rosenberg and D.K. Wilgus for pointing out these analogues to me. The first four tunes are discussed in James J. Fuld, *The Book of World-Famous Music: Classical, Popular and Folk*, rev. ed. (New York: Crown Publishers, 1971), pp. 515-516. "Sink the Bismark" is by the country and western singer Johnny Horton and can be heard on *Johnny Horton's Greatest Hits*, 12 inch, 33 1/3 rpm phono disc, Columbia CL-1596 (n.p., c. 1960). This tune has also been found in the repertoire of at least one traditional fiddler in Newfoundland, Rufus Guinchard, MUNFLA 66-24/CL 74.

[12]I am indebted to Ron MacEachern for pointing out this song to me. See Greenleaf and Mansfield, p. 151; and Wilf and Christine Doyle, *The Mighty Churchill*, 12 inch 33 1/3 rpm phonodisc, London EBX-4157 (Conception Harbour, Nfld., c. 1970).

[13]This information is from a taped interview with Doyle conducted by I. Sheldon Posen and Michael Taft in Conception Harbour, 15 October 1972, MUNFLA 73-45/C1433-1436.

[14]This tale has been found in the repertoires of tellers for at least five hundred years and its popularity is widespread, both in Europe and North America. See Robert C. Cosbey, "The Mak Story and Its Folklore Analogues," *Speculum*, 20 (1945), 310-317.

[15]MUNFLA 74-125, collecting card. RCMP is the abbreviation for Royal Canadian Mounted Police.

[16]Caroline (Broome) Leopold, *The History of New Ross in the County of Lunenburg, Nova Scotia* (New Ross: Committee in Charge, 150th Anniversary of New Ross, 1966), p. 58.

[17]MUNFLA 70-12-p. 180. "Switchel and Dry" refer to weak tea and dry bread which the poachers dined on in jail.

[18]John White, ed., *Burke's Ballads* (St. John's: n. p., 1960?), p. 50.

[19]William Kirwin has recently pointed out the popularity of humorous curse songs, both in Ireland and Newfoundland, in "The Influence of Ireland on the Printed Newfoundland Ballad," in *Literature and Folk Culture: Ireland and Newfoundland*, ed. Alison Feder and Bernice Schrank (St. John's: Memorial Univ. of Newfoundland, 1977), pp. 140-143.

[20]White, pp. 52-53.

[21]MUNFLA, 65-1, pp. 28-29.

[22]Kenneth Peacock, ed., *Songs of the Newfoundland Outports*, Bulletin No. 197, Anthropological Series No. 65 (Ottawa: National Museum of Canada, 1965), p. 78.

[23]*The Mighty Churchill*; and *More Roving*, 12 inch 33 1/3 rpm phonodisc, Audat 477-9014 (Halifax, 1972), respectively.

[24]*Vikings of the Ice: Being the Log of a Tenderfoot on the Great Newfoundland Seal Hunt* (1924; rpt. as *The Greatest Hunt in the World*, Montreal: Tundra Books, 1969), pp. 130-131.

[25]The term "scoff" also has the broader meaning of any impromptu meal, or any meal in which the food is particularly good or abundant.

[26]For a discussion of the scoff in relation to calendar customs, see James C. Faris, *Cat Harbour: A Newfoundland Fishing Settlement*, Newfoundland Social and Economic Studies, No. 3, rev. ed. (St. John's: Institute of Social and Economic Research, Memorial Univ. of Nfld., 1972), pp. 162-163.

[27]MUNFLA 69-5, p. 105. The belief that cats will try to injure the dead or steal the soul is well documented in Wayland D. Hand, ed., *Popular Beliefs and Superstitions from North Carolina*, The Frank C. Brown Collection of North Carolina Folklore, Vol. 7 (Durham: Duke Univ. Press, 1954), belief no. 5427.

[28]MUNFLA 74-126, collecting card.

[29]MUNFLA Q68-282-2.

[30]"A Generic Approach to the Practical Joke," *Southern Folklore Quarterly*, 38 (1974), 260-261.

[31]"Three Charged in Connection with Theft of Vegetables," *Evening Telegram* (St. John's), 2 Oct. 1975, p. 2.

[32]"The Real Thing!" *Daily News* (St. John's), 6 Oct. 1975, p. 1. Ellipsis is sic.

[33]Bernard Brown, "Shot Stealing Apples," *Daily News* (St. John's), 22 Sept. 1975, p. 1.

[34]For a definitive study of threatening figures in Newfoundland, see John D. A. Widdowson, "Aspects of Traditional Verbal Control Threats and Threatening Figures in

Newfoundland Folklore," (unpublished Ph.D. dissertation, Memorial Univ. of Nfld., 1972).

[35]MUNFLA 70-25, p. 24.

[36]MUNFLA 70-24, pp. 20-21.

[37]MUNFLA 70-21, p. 138.

[38]Dick Nolan believes that the popularity of the song is due primarily to this theme.

[39]MUNFLA 69-25, p. 153.

[40]MUNFLA 70-19, p. 78.

[41]*D.P. Newfie*, 12 inch 33 1/3 rpm phonodisc, Audat 477-9017 (St. John's?, 1972); *My Newfoundland Home*, 12 inch 33 1/3 rpm phonodisc, Audat 477-9044 (St. John's, 1973); *You Can't Fool a Newfoundlander*, 12 inch 33 1/3 rpm phonodisc, Marathon ALS-367 (Toronto?, 1973), respectively.

[42]*Happy Newfoundlanders* 12 inch 33 1/3 rpm phonodisc, RCA NCLI-0012 (Toronto, 1973).

[43]*You Can't Fool a Newfoundlander.*

[44]*Drifter From the Coast*, 12 inch 33 1/3 rpm phonodisc, Audat 477-9057 (St. John's, 1973).

[45]*All Aboard for Newfoundland*, 12 inch 33 1/3 phonodisc, Marathon ALS-392 (Toronto?, 1973).

[46]For several years I have asked almost every Newfoundlander I have met if they have heard the song at "times," and those who have regularly attended times in their communities have all agreed that "Aunt Martha's Sheep" is sung at such occasions.

[47]"Song and Singing Traditions at Children's Summer Camps" (unpublished M.A. thesis, Memorial Univ. of Nfld., 1974), p. 154.

[48]Taped interview with Scammell conducted by I. Sheldon Posen and Michael Taft in St. John's, 23 Oct. 1972, MUNFLA 73-45/C1439-1440.

[49]Unpublished TS, n.d. A copy is in the possession of the Reference Division of the Newfoundland Public Library.

[50]C.L. Bennet, J.F. Swayze and Lorne Pierce, *The Golden Caravan*, rev. ed. (Toronto: Ryerson Press and Macmillan Co., 1948), pp. 452-471.

[51]Performed in Carbonear, 9 April 1976.

Rumors of Maggie:
Outlaw News in Folklore

James Hornby

BY NOW, just about everyone has experienced the intensity of public interest in the doings of Margaret Trudeau. In 1980, as I write, public opinion seems to be that she is addicted to media attention, neurotically self-obsessed, and flagrantly indiscreet. Writing at the end of the previous decade, the late Norman DePoe observed that "one might have called the '70s 'The Rise and Fall of Maggie Trudeau' from the starry eyed Camelot-kissed bride of 1971 to the confused, shabby 'personality' she has become— or been revealed."[1] Her best-selling autobiography, *Beyond Reason*,[2] published in April 1979, appeared in such a blaze of sensationalist publicity that it was frequently cited as a reason for the federal election defeat suffered by Pierre Trudeau and the Liberal party in the next month; Trudeau's choice of a wife was seen to reflect negatively upon his judgment in general.[3] Even the woman who interviewed Margaret for *Playgirl*— hardly the raunchiest magazine that featured her in 1979—reportedly said of her: "she's the kind of woman you'd like to run, not walk, to a really good therapist."[4]

The materials for this paper were collected in New Brunswick, Newfoundland and Prince Edward Island, from 1977 to 1979. Most of them were gathered within a year of the Trudeaus' separation (announced May 27, 1977); at this time, Pierre Trudeau was Prime Minister of Canada, and therefore the target of many frustrations, while opinions about Margaret were at first polarized. Her highly-publicized departure was applauded by those who felt she represented the new independence of contemporary women. Several years later, there seems to be a consensus that she is "a household embarrassment";[5] the hurt she has caused her husband, and the effect of her exploits on their growing children, have been major themes in media comments on her lately.[6]

Some of the things Canadians have been saying about her privately are in the form of patterned narratives which circulate widely by word of mouth, and, like other kinds of folklore, vary with the telling. These contemporary items of verbal lore are what I have termed "outlaw news"[7]—jokes and opinions that elaborate upon the mass media information that gives them an impetus.

It must be stated that my collection of these materials was neither scientific nor systematic; indeed, part of it was retrospective. I simply asked people with whom I came in contact if they had heard any stories or jokes about Margaret Trudeau. My collectanea, therefore, is illustrative rather than comprehensive, and presumably there are other items on the same subject.

However, the ones I have found seem to serve the purpose of this paper, which is to illuminate an identity voyage through the use of contemporary folklore and popular culture concerning Margaret Trudeau. Several concepts are crucial here, the first being the "identity voyage" as proposed by Orrin E. Klapp to designate vicarious experience through celebrities. "Identification," says Klapp, "is the psychic mechanism on which one rides."[8] I will not review Margaret's career as I assume, mass media being what they are, that most of us have received the same information about it. Of course, not all of our identity voyages have been the same.

A second underlying concept is that mass media operate on the basis of exchange value rather than truth value, as the motives behind them are pecuniary rather than philosophical. With rare exceptions, their goal is not to inform as well as possible but to attract as large an audience as possible, for the size of the audience—the commodity in the equation—usually determines the rate at which it can be sold to advertisers.[9] Karl Jaspers would probably have seen the exchange basis of media as a result of what he called massification. In *Man in the Modern Age* (1931) he noted: "The divorce of labour from pleasure deprives life of its possible gravity: public affairs become mere entertainment."[10] Similarly, C.W.E. Bigsby has written that modern alienation.

is the condition . . . of maximum receptivity to a mass art, ideal for the production and consumption of a popular culture that no longer links man to his own past but which provides a temporary connection across class in the present.[11]

Whatever the reason, I want to emphasize that modern technological media have elevated gossip (which is itself often described in terms of its social exchange value for such goals as prestige[12]) to such a level that it has almost become invisible in the McLuhanistic sense of a pervasive environment. In the global village we have global gossip. Or as José Ortega y Gasset, a McLuhanist before McLuhan, wrote in *The Revolt of the Masses* (1930):

Life has become, in actual fact, world-wide in character. I mean that the content of existence for the average man of today includes the whole planet; that each individual habitually lives the life of the whole world.[13]

Through their ability to diffuse images over great distances almost instantaneously, mass media can bombard many of those who are uninterested or even unwilling to receive its latest celebrity messages. In the case of Margaret Trudeau, one observer has said that she sold her autobiography "to those who kept saying they couldn't stand hearing anything more about her."[14] As Daniel Boorstin states, "the power to make a reportable event is ... the power to make experience."[15] This function of the media is what produces fame, since a story or a new face with a good "angle" usually creates a bandwagon effect among competing media. For instance, the appearance of rock musician Bruce Springsteen on the covers of *Time* and *Newsweek* in the same period in 1975 had the intrinsic effect (through the influence of these magazines on their readers) and extrinsic effect (through their influence on other magazines and media) of making him an instant star and celebrity, although he was previously known to a relatively small audience.

The circular, self-contained nature of the etiology of such celebrity is that it is a media fiction which through the potency of media becomes a fact. Such is the nature of present-day fame. As John Lahr has written:

Fame is changing. Visibility is now an end in itself. A celebrity in our media-dominated age is, in Daniel Boorstin's words, "someone who is famous for being well-known."[16]

Or, to quote Boorstin again, the celebrity is "the human pseudo-event."[17]

It is in the context of the above that I will discuss the relationship of folklore and mass culture to Margaret Trudeau's quantum leap in celebrity in 1977. As represented in folklore collected in Atlantic Canada and probably circulated nationally, she took many Canadians on an identity voyage of humiliation of her husband. This national voyage of scandal and humiliation had two main components: 1) It seems that Margaret's humiliation of Pierre inspired others to take part in his discomfiture; 2) In the song, jokes and stories I have gathered from oral circulation, she is also an object of ridicule, although initially less so than Pierre.[18]

Considering the twenty-nine years difference in their ages, it is not surprising that a large component of the public in which the material emphasizing Pierre's humiliation was found was closer to her age than his. It is probable that her assertion of independence and dramatic exit struck a chord of sympathy and identity among many young people (not just women), especially during the high state of collective excitement the country was in during March through May 1977, when the extent of their differences became public.

The publicity given these events provided ideal occasions for slandering Prime Minister Trudeau, which of course is an occupational hazard of public office. It is interesting to speculate, though it is beyond the scope of this inquiry, that the relish with which Trudeau's embarrassment was reflected in folklore indicates a national streak of masochism, and follows feelings of loss and disillusionment. Indeed, Pierre Trudeau's position seems analogous to what Sir James Frazer called "The Burden of Royalty" in *The Golden Bough*:

The idea that early kingdoms are despotisms in which the people exist only for the sovereign is wholly inapplicable to the monarchies we are considering. On the contrary, the sovereign in them exists only for his subjects; his life is valuable so long as he discharges the duties of his position by ordering the course of nature for his people's benefit. So soon as he fails to do so, the care, the devotion, the religious homage which they had hitherto lavished on him cease and are changed into hatred and contempt.[19]

Likewise, through his image of aloofness as Prime Minister during a recession, Trudeau was a man many Canadians loved to hate.

Yet during the glorious public honeymoon of the first few years of his marriage, before inflation and factionalism reached levels that eroded the nation's morale, there was a fairy tale quality to Pierre Trudeau's image. Part of his later downslide in public esteem may have been related to the novelty wearing off his marriage; with the apparent collapse of his marriage, he has regained some of his popularity.

Certainly his marriage had legendary elements. It seemed more than the symbolic entry of the children of the Sixties into the power elite—it was taken to be a form of homeopathic magic that united the old and the new, emergent Canada. The birth of the Trudeaus' first two children on Christmas Day (Justin Pierre James in 1971 and Alexandre Emmanuel "Sacha" in 1973) seemed fitting proof of a mythical union. Significantly, it was at this period that Trudeau announced Quebec separatism was dead.

The popular culture and folklore elements herein discussed consist of a song and several jokes and short narratives that I collected in the Atlantic Provinces, 1977-79; most of the collecting was done within a year of the Trudeaus' separation. It is not possible to say how representative they are of Canadian public opinion generally, but many of them seem to have had wide circulation.

*   *

The symbiotic relationship that folkloric interaction and the mass media can have is well illustrated by the oral circulation of a song entitled "Margaret," released on a 45 r.p.m. record by Condor Records of Toronto. This was an opportunistic topical parody that associated the Trudeaus' marital misfortunes with an extremely successful record, one of the top sellers in 1977, a country tearjerker called "Lucille." The parody "Margaret" was collected several times during the summer of 1978 by students doing fieldwork for the Newfoundland Folk Arts Council, and at least one complete version was thus obtained from oral sources.[20]

One striking aspect of the popularity of this record when it was current was that it seemed to be more widespread in oral circulation than from its primary mass medium, radio, where it was not available for very long. Many stations never played it; others, like VOCM, a powerful AM station in St. John's, Newfoundland, aired it for a short time before it was banned.[21]

Yet while living in Fredericton, New Brunswick, in 1977, I can remember hearing people singing the chorus of "Margaret." They seemed to especially enjoy their imitations of the caricature of Pierre Trudeau's voice in that part of the recording. Many persons I talked to then and since also heard of the recording only through oral report or performance, never on radio.

Information obtained from several radio stations in St. John's indicates that "Margaret" was considered a hot item in the trade, and was handled very carefully. An announcer at CHOZ-FM said his station played it but a few times before "the word came down to haul it off the air, so they hauled it off in a hurry." The program director at VOCM said there were "legal hassles about it" and it was "pulled off the market."[22]

The paper sleeve on the copy of this record that I obtained from VOCM clearly shows how this station treated it. First, it does not have filing numbers on it, as the record was not playlisted, but just left around the control room. Second, instructions to the disc jockeys are written clearly on the sleeve (see photo) and these instructions speak for themselves.

The story from the broadcast industry perspective is told concisely in *RPM Weekly*, the Canadian recording industry's trade and charts paper. In the May 28, 1977 issue was this breezy note:

You talk about your timely and red-hot parodies . . . . Margaret, written and sung by CFGM air personality Frank Proctor is in heavy demand with commercially recorded copies of the take-off on Lucille just released 5/16 on the Condor label. As you may have gathered, Margaret is based on the recent goings-on in the Trudeau household in particular and the Canadian political scene in general.

The story also indicated that Proctor had been encouraged by the response of his parody when originally broadcast on CFGM, Toronto.

A month later, in *RPM*'s June 25, 1977 issue, there was the strange headline, "Publisher forces Condor to stop pressing Maggie," and this story:

U.S. publishing firm Brougham Hall have forbidden the pressing of any more copies of novelty single Margaret by CFGM morning man Frank Proctor. The single is a take-off on international hit Lucille, which is published by Brougham Hall. It deals with Margaret Trudeau, and purports to be sung by Pierre Crudeau and Bob Stammerfield.[23]

After a review of the success of "Lucille" the article concludes:

Condor reports the move by the publisher will have a substantial effect on them, as the single has already sold over 2,000 units with orders for additional product. These orders will be left unfulfilled.

Here are the words to "Margaret" as transcribed from the recording:

In a bar in the capital across from the Rideau
On a barstool she took off her rings
I thought I'd get closer so I walked on over
I sat down and asked her her name
When the drinks finally hit her she said I'm no quitter
But I've finally quit living on dreams
I'm hungry for laughter and here ever after
I'm after whatever photography brings.

In the mirror I saw him and I closely watched him
Rose petals a droopy disgrace
He came to the woman and sat down beside her
He had a strange look on his face
He was carrying Pampers some arrowroot cookies
Dishpan hands were swollen and red
But he started shakin' and she started a-quakin'
He turned to the woman and said:

Chorus
You picked a fine time to leave me Margaret
Three hungry children and I'm losing Quebec
Sure I've got Horner but I can't hug Horner
And whaddya mean "wanna bet?"
You picked a fine time to leave me Margaret.

After he left us I ordered more Pepsi
I thought how she'd made him look small
From the lights of the Rideau he climbed in his limo
And sat without talkin' at all
She was a beauty a real camera cutie
She wanted to snap one of me
An eight-by-ten glossy but oh she's too bossy
'Sides she's framed poor Pierre can't ya see:

(Then two choruses, with the final "Margaret" spoken; then a spoken tag, in the "Stammerfield" voice: "Ah, oh Maggie, ya take group rates? uh, photos you know for albums, I'd like to get some for the kids and family myself, I'd vote for you, yeah, huh, oh sure, sign me up Margaret (belch)")[24]

A historical note: Jack Horner crossed the floor of the House of Commons to join Trudeau's Liberal party in April 1977. *RPM* stated that "Margaret" was commercially released on May 16.

As can be seen from an examination of its words, the song parodies the Trudeaus' marital problems in the form of low burlesque.[25] While the great interest in their situation and the spectacle of Trudeau singing a country-and-western sob story are risque and unusual enough to account for the record's novelty appeal, the elements that made it worth learning and performing to others indicate a folkloric response to what Margaret called "my ultimate freedom trip."[26]

I suggest four reasons for this song's entry into oral circulation: 1) the song ridicules the high and mighty, providing what Tamotsu Shibutani calls a kind of wish fulfillment;[27] 2) there is a resurrection of the once commonly verbalized suggestion that Pierre is sexually inclined toward men—thus the song reinforces an established piece of folklore; 3) there is the implication of a national insecurity about Confederation that largely dates from the election of the separatist Parti Quebecois in Quebec in November 1976; 4) parody is a popular sub-genre in Atlantic Canada.[28] However, in the case of "Margaret" the parody was not created or adapted, but simply learned. Thus it is not a folk parody, but the folk use of a parody, as it was transmitted orally to a large extent.

When one considers the first of my four reasons for this occurrence, it is clear that while both Margaret and Pierre are ridiculed, Pierre fares much worse. The caricature of Trudeau singing a country-and-western song with weepy pedal-steel guitar backup is ridiculous by itself, not only because of Pierre's public office but because he has usually been seen as intellectually aloof and emotionally restrained. His personal motto, "Le raison avant la passion,"[29] exemplifies this quality. Much of the shock arising from Margaret's well-publicized visits with the Rolling Stones can be traced to what we might call a contrast in paradigms—her choice of "la passion" (presumably the Stones' motto is the reverse of Pierre's) over "le raison." The title of her best-selling autobiography, *Beyond Reason*, also seems to refer to this motto.

Details of the lyric give a degrading portrait of Pierre. As a symbol of his mental state, the line "Rose petals a droopy disgrace" contrasts with his usual natty boutonniere, and is reminiscent of Margaret's much-quoted statement, "I'm going to be more than just a rose in my husband's lapel."[30] The portrait of the Prime Minister as a deserted and hapless house-husband—"He was carrying Pampers, some arrowroot cookies, dishpan hands were swollen and red"—extends the same theme.

The ridicule of Margaret in the song is relatively minor: "When the drinks finally hit her" and "she's too bossy" are instances; another is the sexual innuendo of the spoken question, "ya take group rates?" which may be a reference to the Rolling Stones. Overall, though, she is portrayed as happier and freer than her husband. The irony of her self-proclaimed "escape" from public pressures is that an American song ("Lucille") was used as a basis for comment on her escape to America. This side of the story was neatly encapsulated by Ben Wicks' syndicated cartoon that showed her in a doctor's office, with the doctor saying, "try getting away from the public eye, Margaret. Spend a few days in New York."[31] A related irony is that the most shocking and "newsworthy" statements she made in New

York were published in the American gossip magazine *People*. As Lahr observes, "fame has become America's greatest export."[32]

In the second element of the song's appeal, the imputation that Trudeau is sexually inclined toward men resurfaces in the self-explanatory lines, "sure I've got Horner, but I can't hug Horner/And whaddya mean, wanna bet?"

Thirdly, as a touchstone for national insecurity, I believe that the incongruous line "three hungry children and I'm losing Quebec" is a joking way of voicing anxiety about the future of the country. As *RPM* noted, the record is also about "the Canadian political scene in general."[33]

It is significant that all of the above elements are found only in the chorus, which is the part of the song that circulated widely through oral transmission. Another factor is that the complete song was not easily heard because of limited commercial availability and airplay on radio. So the whole song must have been difficult to learn without special effort and some luck, but the parody of the familiar "Lucille" chorus was readily memorable. (This song may be the one referred to in a Canadian Press story from Toronto not long before the May 22, 1979 election which noted that "the band the Conservatives used to warm up audiences was ordered to stop using a song lampooning Margaret after it had been sung only once."[34])

*   *   *

Although the first of the following two jokes concerning Margaret was widely recounted, I collected them together in a taped interview with two informants at Memorial University of Newfoundland in February 1978:

Informant 1:
The joke which I heard last spring sometime was that, uh, the Trudeaus were building a patio and, uh, Pierre is mixing the cement and Margaret is laying the stones. Right?
Informant 2:
The one I heard was that this was the reason they were going to break up, the fact that the marriage was in trouble and that . . . Pierre tried to poison her and gave her a piece of meat that was over fifty years old.
Informant 1:
That's very similar to the joke about, uh, Jackie, Jackie Kennedy and the wedding gift from Aristotle Onassis—an antique pendant.[35] This is the same sort of thing.
Interviewer:
Yeah, well, some people thought that, uh, Margaret Trudeau was going to be or was the Canadian Jackie Kennedy. So.

Informant 1 reported telling the Stones/stones-laying joke at a convention in 1977 and said:

A lot of people had heard it, or had variants of it, but I don't remember what the variants were. It was definitely quite on the go last spring.

Both of these jests are essentially one-liners at Pierre's expense. The first is on a cuckold theme, while the second comments unfavorably on the age difference between the couple. Both are hostile toward Pierre.

A narrative I heard several times in fragmentary form also implies that Pierre was cuckolded. The story concerns a message (none of my informants remembered what) written in the snow outside the Prime Minister's residence. Upon inquiring about it, Pierre is told that it has been tested and "the urine belongs to Mick Jagger of the Rolling Stones; but the handwriting is Margaret's."[36]

Another narrative was recounted as follows:

Interviewer:
You said something about, you heard a story of why Margaret left Pierre.
Informant:
Yeah, well first of all you have to be familiar with Pierre's political moves, and the basic premise is that Pierre is going to turn Canada into an entirely French nation, and you can tell this first by his bilingualism program, but more importantly by the introduction of metrification into Canada as a whole.
Interviewer:
So we're all going to hell in a metric handcart.
Informant:
Yes, exactly. Now the thing is that Margaret understands, understood, uh, Pierre's plan you see, and disagreed with it. Now they had some fights over this matter before she left, but this was the cause of the split—she simply could not live with a person whose plan was to turn Canada into a French country.
Interviewer:
So there's no real punch line.
Informant:
No, there's no real punch line.
Interviewer:
Margaret was the people's advocate.
Informant:
Yes.[37]

I note that the anti-French theme, which emerges explicitly here, is also suggested by the line from the song, "after he left us, I ordered more Pepsi." "Pepsi" is a *blason populaire* that denotes a person of French background; it is common in eastern Canada, especially in Quebec. In this case the element of ethnic xenophobia is more prominent than a personal dislike for Pierre.

Despite what he may have lost, it seems that Pierre has gained a lot of sympathy and respect since the separation, although the folklore noted above indicates otherwise. Those materials however, were all collected in

1977-78. Since then Trudeau's personal and party fortunes have improved: a Liberal general election victory returned him as Prime Minister, and the three "Margaret" jokes I heard in 1979 show a greater respect for Pierre and less respect for the woman known by the revealing journalistic cliché as his "estranged wife." All were unsolicited, and were noted down as accurately as possible shortly after I heard them.

The first was in a simple question-and-answer form:

Q: What has the most fingerprints—the RCMP, CIA or MTA?
A: MTA—Margaret Trudeau's ass.[38]

This I heard only once; it came from the most active bearer of current jokes that I have met. It is clearly scornful of Mrs. Trudeau's morals. The laughter it excited in the gathering where I heard it seemed to be an expression of agreement with the put-down rather than a real appreciation of the "jest."

The second item was first overheard in a bar, and subsequently told several times by people who knew of my interest in the subject. It is also in question-and-answer form:

Q: What do Margaret Trudeau and Maureen McTeer have in common?
A: They both like to blow a little dope.[39]

This is really more of a veiled "Joe Clark" joke than anything else. There have been a number of jokes about the former Progressive Conservative leader who briefly replaced Trudeau as Prime Minister, mostly of the "numbskull" type.

The final item, basically a one-liner, obviously derived from news reports that Margaret claimed to have had an affair with U.S. Senator Edward Kennedy. Here is the basic form of this joke, also heard several times:

Margaret calls Pierre to say that she's having an affair with Senator Kennedy. Pierre replies, "Ask him to drive you home."[40]

This, again, manages to comment cruelly on several public figures at once. The punch line of course refers to the Chappaquiddick incident that has haunted Kennedy's career. But primarily it expresses a desire to hear no more of publicity-hungry Margaret.

*   *   *

"Fame is the perversion of the natural human instinct for validation and attention," according to English playwright Heathcote Williams.[41] However, attention does not imply validation.

An example of the range of opinions once held about Margaret Trudeau are two letters to the editor of the January 23, 1978 issue of *People*. Wrote S. Evans (Tempe, Arizona), "I see Margaret as a warm, caring young woman. I also understand completely why she feels she must do this at this time in her life." Jane Ford, of Hamilton, Ontario, riposted, "why doesn't someone tell Margaret Trudeau to shut up. Every time she opens her mouth, she embarrasses the entire country." Clearly these women were on different identity voyages, and assimilated this event differently into their lives.

The second letter underlines the fact that the folklore I have collected on this subject merely reports on one of an infinite variety of chains of transmission. Certainly many Canadians identified more with Pierre from the beginning, as he had to put up with humiliation and extra responsibility while Margaret acquired freedom and celebrity status. Symbolic of these were the numerous published photographs of her dancing at a trendy Manhattan disco. (Here it is ironic to recall that in her first public appearance as Mrs. Trudeau, on a 1971 state visit to Russia, Margaret "made a solo visit to the Bolshoi Ballet School, whose director told her she would make a good gypsy dancer."[42]) She became famous by stepping outside the mold of her role as Mrs. Prime Minister, which may explain the gross and cruel folklore she stimulated. One cannot imagine similar material being circulated about Maryon Pearson, who said of her husband, Trudeau's predecessor Lester B. Pearson, "I married him for better or for worse—not just for lunch."[43] The difference is that Margaret was willing to take radical action against what she saw as the cause of her dissatisfaction. Identification with or against her actions polarized public opinion.

Perhaps the line in the "Margaret" song, "three hungry children and I'm losing Quebec" is not so incongruous after all—for Margaret's "abdication" as she called it,[44] seemed at one period to have as much impact in the media as Quebec separatism. Like the Parti Quebecois, Margaret was willing to risk disintegration and pay the price.

If Canada deserves Robertson Davies' characterization as "The Daughter Who Stayed at Home," Margaret was well cast as the daughter who ran away. Barbara Amiel has observed in *Maclean's* that "Margaret's behavior had been a matter of national scrutiny from the day of her wedding and Canadians responded to the final throes of her marriage as if they had been collectively cuckolded."[45] (This may suggest psychological reasons for the folklore emphasizing Trudeau being cuckolded.) Amiel wrote that, if nothing else, Margaret has *chutzpah*, which is presumably what many women identified with.

Several writers have held her up as a true product of the Sixties style of narcissism. Others have noted that hers is a *success de scandale* and not a *success d'estime,* but as everyone from Francis Bacon ("Fame is like a river, that beareth up things light and swoln, and drowns things weighty and solid"[46]) to John Lahr has remarked, the classical idea of fame as reputation based on accomplishment no longer holds; now "gesture replaces commitment."[47]

In the case of Margaret Trudeau, the gesture was seen by writers in many ways, though never quite as in the folklore I have presented. Since a range of attitudes on the subject was explored in the media, the orally structured and transmitted forms express a type of opinion that the technological mass media could not or would not handle. The boundaries of this division may be illustrated by the handling of the record "Margaret."

As a sidelight to this media fallout, I remember seeing, in the fall of 1977, an ad for a new brand of jeans for women called "Maggie T's" (note the pun in the name). The ad featured a hind view photo reminiscent of the "tight jeans" photo of Margaret in her first sensational *People* magazine interview[48]—and a camera. I have found no evidence that they were sold for long, but the fact that they were marketed indicates the level of popular identification with the implicit subject. Their apparent failure may have been because the identification was not as strongly positive as the merchants had estimated.

This is not to suggest that more sophisticated observations about Margaret in the media did not contain ridicule and malice—but they were higher-toned in expression. Thus, in the *New Republic,* Roger Rosenblatt questioned, "why do we enjoy reading of the escapades of the mighty?"[49] Auberon Waugh wrote in the *Spectator* that Mrs. Trudeau is both insane (as evidenced by her breakdown in 1974) and selfish.[50] What he found odd about the publicity she received is that:

Mrs. Trudeau is seen as a typical, healthy child of her generation. If she has been inside a psychiatric hospital, so have a large proportion of women in her class and age-group. Her egotistical ravings . . . are the feminine small-talk of innumerable middle-class London dinner parties. I have scarcely sat next to a woman in the last ten years who has not told me in the course of the meal that she is in pursuit of her own self, that she finds the pressure to conform, to do things she doesn't want to do, really too much, too much, that her artistic integrity requires greater freedom for its self expression.

He added: "Many people seem to be troubled by the stirrings of an artistic impulse nowadays. I do not suppose there has been a moment in the world's history when more people felt themselves to be artists, or when less art was produced." As for Pierre, said Waugh, anyone could have told him the marriage would never work, but "it was just a question of the price he was prepared to pay for cutting a little dash—one more reminder of the glorious fact that sex makes fools of us all."[51]

While I would say that the sort of folklore discussed here is on a lower expressive plane than Waugh's remarks, they are similar in the use of ridicule. We may conclude that they represent different constituencies that are on different identity voyages, and revere dissimilar symbols and ideals. It seems that all forms of communication have a bias, whether political, generational or attitudinal. As Shibutani wrote in a 1962 article, "each social world, then, is a culture area, the boundaries of which are set neither by territory nor formal group membership, but by the limits of effective communication."[52]

It is in the nature of celebrities that they are often attacked by the media for using the status that popular attention has given them, especially after they have rejected the image or role by which they acquired it. For these role expectations seem not merely reported by the media but developed and reified by them in the public mind. As Rosnow and Fine observe, in public life, "the line between relevant information and titillating gossip is a thin one."[53] I would say this is true of any medium, including this one. But Rosnow and Fine, and John Lahr as well, see this not as an inherent fact of human communication but as an effect of mass media. Norman Mailer has coined the term "factoids" to describe certain media creations: "facts which have no existence before appearing in a magazine or newspaper, creations which are not so much likes as a product to manipulate emotions in the Silent Majority."[54] Or, as Rosnow and Fine write, in media "it is difficult to separate information from entertainment, hard fact from rumor, significant information from gossip—which 'conditions' the public to a superficial level of cognition."[55] Lahr sees the same phenomenon:

Means and ends are confused in the public mind when killers and kings are seen to reap the same celebrity status, when public malefactors are rewarded for their notoriety with the accoutrements of success. Fame legitimizes greed by making it glorious.

Lahr begins his piece by quoting an Associated Press dispatch on a hostage incident where the gunman's "only demand has been to hold a press conference."[56] Within the exchange values of media, the pay-off is attention. As Oscar Wilde once observed, "the only bad public notice is an obituary."

Many structured forms of expressive culture are anti-celebrity in the sense that very negative public notices are frequently given, while in forms like latrinalia, and its verbal relations, coarseness is *de rigueur*. Such forms express frustrations that celebrities do not live up to the role expectations of a given taste group when they fail to provide an identity voyage that would satisfy this group. As Klapp has observed:

The "Mitty" function is conspicuous in the mass use of celebrities—compensating people for what they cannot do themselves (always, then, symbolizing a certain amount of frustration, even in vicarious gratification).[57]

Like celebrities, folklore can be a lightning rod for frustration by expressing "outsider" opinions or minority issues which do not get much hearing in other forms of communication.

Presumably Pierre Trudeau, who as Justice Minister was widely quoted as saying that the state has no business in the bedrooms of the nation, feels the reverse is true as well. But gossip, which includes rumor, fact and factoid in a complex and shifting mixture, cannot be locked out. Since the pervasiveness of technological media and popular culture and the vagueness of the line between fact and rumor provides both official news and what Shibutani calls "improvised news"—rumors that arise in response to a need for more information than is officially available—the collective folkloric formation of improvised news happens in conjunction with mass media. Only in what might be called "outlaw news"—wild speculations or jokes presented as the "real" truth (often satirically)—does folklore have the field largely to itself.

However one assesses the social benefits of these communications, they at least suggest that public opinion is not fixed or limited by mass media. For although many oral forms interact with the content of mass media, the folklore which results is traditional in its expressive forms and freedoms. Such folklore, representing an *ad hoc* taste public, can indicate much about the sort of identity voyages some people take.[58]

Notes

[1]From DePoe's review of *Farewell to the 70s* by Anna Porter and Marjorie Harris. Circulated by Canadian Press, it appeared in the Charlottetown *Guardian*, Dec. 29, 1979, 4.

[2]Margaret Trudeau, *Beyond Reason* (London: Paddington Press, 1979).

[3]See, for example, *Maclean's* magazine's March 26, 1979 cover story, "The Margaret Factor," by Judith Timson and Allan Fotheringham's end-page column in its April 30, 1979 issue.

[4]Quoted in *Maclean's* "People" section, Aug. 20, 1979, p. 28.

[5]*Ibid.*

[6]See Jane O'Hara's "Bedtime Story: the wife is always the last to know," *Maclean's*, Dec. 3, 1979; and letters to the editor of the Toronto *Star* (Aug. 18, 1979), p. B-3.

[7]Since I first used this term, Peter Narváez has alerted me to a parallel use of the term "outlaw" by Fred E.H. Schroeder in his *Outlaw Aesthetics: Arts and the Popular Mind* (Bowling Green, Ohio: Bowling Green University Popular Press, 1977). While Schroeder's focus is more on aesthetics than communications, he is speaking to my concerns in this

passage: "...it appears that popular aesthetic standards are always outlaw aesthetics, by which I mean that popular tastes will assert themselves regardless of how much they are opposed and repressed, how much the people are instructed, or how much they are given an elevated aesthetic diet upon which to feed" (pp. 8-9).

[8]Orrin E. Klapp, Collective Search for Identity (New York: Holt, Rinehart & Winston, 1969), p. 213.

[9]For an articulate expression of this concept as it relates to advertising see Jules Henry, "Advertising as a Philosophical System," in his Culture Against Man (New York: Vintage Books, 1963), pp. 45-99.

[10]Karl Jaspers, Man in the Modern Age, trans. Eden and Cedar Paul (London: Routledge and Kegan Paul, 1951), p. 37.

[11]C.W.E. Bigsby, "The Politics of Popular Culture," in Bigsby, ed., Approaches to Popular Culture (London: Edward Arnold, 1976), p. 9.

[12]See, for example, Ralph L. Rosnow and Gary Alan Fine, Rumor and Gossip: The Social Psychology of Hearsay (New York: Elsevier, 1976), passim.

[13]José Ortega y Gasset, The Revolt of the Masses (New York: Norton, 1957), p. 38.

[14]Roy McGregor, in Maclean's "People" section, Dec. 31, 1979.

[15]Daniel J. Boorstin, The Image: A Guide to Pseudo-Events in America (New York: Atherton, 1971), p. 10.

[16]John Lahr, "Notes on Fame," Harper's, Jan. 1978, p. 77.

[17]Boorstin, p. 57.

[18]But in other areas, such as being the subject of such undignified drivel as Felicity Cochrane's Margaret Trudeau: The Prime Minister's Runaway Wife (Scarborough, Ont: The New American Library of Canada, Ltd., 1978), Margaret receives more ridicule. She also seems to receive more barbs from comedians, both professional and amateur.

[19]J.G. Frazer, The Golden Bough: A Study in Magic and Religion, abridged edition (London and Basingstoke: Macmillan, 1971), pp. 225-6.

[20]I am indebted to Anne Burke for this information.

[21]This information is from a personal interview with VOCM program director John Reynolds in March 1978.

[22]From interviews I conducted in March 1978.

[23]The inclusion of a Robert Stanfield voice in the parody is patently an excuse to use a "funny" voice on the verses (Trudeau's is on the choruses). Stanfield had by this time stepped down as Leader of the Opposition, but his voice was then more recognizable than that of his successor, Joe Clark.

[24]Bob Stammerfield/Pierre Crudeau [Frank Proctor], "Margaret," one 7" 45 rpm phonodisc (Condor C-97150-A, 1977).

[25]I use this term in the literary sense that distinguishes low burlesque (ridicule achieved by treating something elevated as though it were common) from high burlesque (ridicule by treating the common as if it were elevated).

[26]Arthur Johnson, Margaret Trudeau (Markham, Ont.: Paper Jacks Ltd., 1977), p. 11.

[27]Tamotsu Shibutani, Improvised News: A Sociological Study of Rumor (Indianapolis: Bobbs-Merrill, 1966), p. 86.

[28]As pointed out by Peter Narváez, "The Folk Parodist," Canadian Folk Music Journal, 5 (1977), 32-37, parody has not received its due from students of songmaking traditions in Canada.

[29]Quoted in John Robert Colombo, ed., Colombo's Canadian Quotations (Edmonton: Hurtig Publishers, 1974), p. 594.

[30]Johnson, p. 137.

[31]My copy of this cartoon, from the Toronto Globe & Mail, is unfortunately undated.

[32]Lahr, p. 78.

[33]RPM Weekly, 27:8, p. 36.

[34]Stuart Lake, CP story printed in the St. John's Evening Telegram (April 12, 1979), p. 26.

[35]Gershon Legman, in Rationale of the Dirty Joke, First Series (New York: Grove Press, 1971), p. 618, records earlier versions of this joke. My informants here, and all others not

named, wish anonymity.

36This is a variant of a traditional narrative that appears as the title tale of Vance Randolph's collection *Pissing in the Snow and Other Ozark Folktales* (New York: Avon Books, 1976).

37Taped by me with Penny Houlden in March 1978, at Memorial University of Newfoundland.

38Heard in Georgetown, P.E.I., July 23, 1979.

39Heard in Charlottetown, June 26, 1979.

40Heard in various parts of P.E.I. in 1979.

41Lahr, p.47.

42Quoted in *Life* (June 4, 1971), p. 33.

43*Maclean's* (Nov. 15, 1976), p. 47.

44Johnson, p. 20.

45Barbara Amiel, "Swinging on a star: The coming of age of Margaret Trudeau," *Maclean's* (April 3, 1978), p. 42.

46*The Home Book of Quotations: Classical and Modern* selected and arranged by Burton Stevenson, 10th ed. (New York: Dodd, Mead and Co., 1967), p. 624.

47Lahr, p. 20.

48Robin Leach, "Margaret Trudeau's Manhattan Escape Turns into a Stirring Plea for Freedom," *People* (March 28, 1977), pp. 18-23.

49Roger Rosenblatt, "Maggie and Wilbur," *New Republic* (May 7, 1977), p. 37.

50Rosenblatt found it "unfair" of Waugh to accuse her of both.

51Auberon Waugh, "Found under a Stone," *Spectator* (March 19, 1977), p. 6.

52Tamotsu Shibutani, "Reference Groups and Social Control," in Arnold M. Rose, ed., *Human Behavior and Social Processes: An Interactionist Approach* (Boston: Houghton Mifflin, 1962), p. 136.

53Rosnow and Fine, p. 128.

54Norman Mailer, *Marilyn* (New York: Warner Paperback Library, 1975), p. 21.

55Rosnow and Fine, p. 104.

56Lahr, p. 77.

57Klapp, p. 212.

58An earlier version was delivered at the annual meeting of the Folklore Studies Association of Canada, London, Ontario, June 1978.

Occupational Stereotype, Technique and the Critical Comment of Folklore

Robert S. McCarl

F.C. BARTLETT IN HIS ESSAY on human skill makes the point that each occupation can be typified by its central or key skill—the primary technique upon which success or failure in the work place is measured.[1] In attempting to apply this approach to specific work groups, however, the ethnographer soon finds him or herself with a variety of key techniques required at different times or in different contexts in order to accomplish certain tasks. The central work technique of tool or die making, for example, is the shaping of steel to make die parts using a variety of machines. Yet the vast number of types of tool and die shops alone (job shop, captive shop, research lab shop, garage shop) suggests the need for a closer examination of key techniques within specific contexts prior to the postulation of a metaphorical "key" technique for any one kind of work. By metaphorical key technique I mean the immediate image generated when someone tells us what they do—guns and arrest for policemen, vacuuming for house workers, tightening bolts for assembly line workers, or lecturing for teachers; in other words, what we allow to symbolically stand for activities we really know very little about. The mass media's presentation of occupations and workers and our own popular conceptions of what it is others do for a living is so totally dependent upon these key metaphors that it causes us to stereotype our expectations based on conventionalized occupational symbols. It is the nature of these metaphors and their implications regarding our preconceptions about work and work culture that I intend to explore in this brief discussion— initially by illustrating their generation within an occupational group (smokejumpers) and secondly, their presentation in the mass media and internalization within a specific work context (that of urban fire fighters).

From the "dark satanic mills" of the industrial revolution to Johnny Paychek's popular song "You Can Take This Job and Shove It, I Ain't Working' Here No More," work in general and particularly industrial work has been reviled as a demeaning, exploitative, hell-like experience. Chaplin's little tramp caught between the gears of industry, Red Skelton at the mercy of a maniacal pie production line and film presentations of industrial work like "Norma Rae" and "Silkwood" seem to substantiate this contemporary belief—work is bad and assembly line work is hell. But beyond this general stereotype there lies a complex web of interrelations between people and their specific work experience. Occupational sociologists have identified networks of informal work culture that not only provide for expressive behavior but actually are the necessary social base of any industrial setting.[2] Whether or not we are talking about the personal satisfactions of a combination man who is practicing a variety of craft techniques or the highly stylized and complex levels of sabotage and "government" work that provide a minimal level of self expression for more alienated, anomic workers on the line, there is an expressible network behind the stereotype and it is this level of occupational experience we should be attempting to understand.

In order to appreciate the way in which these key metaphorical stereotypes are employed, we must explore their use between occupational groups that have parallel yet divergent functions, e.g., doctors and lawyers, policemen and fire fighters, lathers and plasterers, letter carriers and clerks, and to take a specific example from my own experience and fieldwork, smokejumpers and ground crew workers who fight forest fires in the Pacific Northwest and in Alaska. Smokejumpers are the "prima donnas" of forest fire attack, relying on parachutes as their means of transportation into isolated areas; while ground crew members (as the name implies) reach the fire usually by bus, truck or on foot. The jumpers are often referred to by the media as the "Green Berets of the Forest Service," as "Young Daredevils Who Leap into the Flaming Jaws of Hell," whereas the ground crew is usually assigned to the arduous and thankless task of digging a fire line around the blaze and mentioned by number in newspaper accounts, if at all.

The jumpers refer to themselves collectively as "jumpers" and to the ground crew as "pounders." The latter refer to themselves as members of a particular suppression crew—the Southfork Crew, the Arboretum Crew or the Redmond Crew, and they refer to the jumpers as "hot dogs." Keeping in mind Fernandez's suggestion that "a sensitive ethnography must obtain the metaphors that men predicate on themselves so as to locate the movements they desire to make in the culture they occupy," we can discern the "movement" of these key metaphors and their linkage to, yet manipulation of, the occupation group they describe.[3]

Outside of their unique mode of transportation, smokejumpers, like other fire fighters, use axes, pulaskis, hoes, shovels, chain saws, etc. to suppress forest fires. The nature of their training and the additional risk of parachuting in the mountains, coupled with the use of jumpers on isolated fires in wilderness areas, provides them with a tremendous *esprit de corps*, individual freedom on a fire, and often an overt feeling of superiority over other fire fighers. The ground crew, on the other hand, works as a unit and if it is a line-building-suppression-crew, they construct fire trail using a synchronized, rhythmic system of progressive trail building that requires each man to dig two feet of bare earth before he stands up, shouts "bump" or "move" and the whole line progresses.

The metaphors employed by both groups are linked to specific behaviors within the occupational experiences of the other, i.e., the jumpers, who as initial attack are usually released when the ground crew arrives on the fire, do appear to be almost totally free to do whatever they want on the fire. Often they wear special bright orange NoMex shirts with the name of their smokejumper base stencilled on the back and generally behave in a manner that appears much more showy than that of the other fire fighters. The ground crew, on the other hand, does attack the fire by pounding the ground with hoes, and from the jumpers' point of view that is an activity that requires little individuality or thought—resulting in the collective designation as pounders.

Although these terms reflect an awareness of the work processes and behaviors of the work group members, they are actually commenting on that aspect of the work which they consider most different from themselves and their approach to a parallel activity, and therefore most in need of what Fernandez would call rhetorical movement.[4] The term "pounder" implies a repetitious, mechanical uniformity which has negative connotations to the individualistic jumpers; while the "hot dog" metaphor suggests a flamboyant aggressiveness which differs from the regimented behavior and effective organization of the ground crew. The movement of these metaphors in their strategic manipulation by members of each group is toward a recognition and confirmation of non-uniformity. Jumpers are flashy and individualistic and ground crews do work as a synchronized unit, but basically they perform the same function in the fire fighting situation and differ only in their mode of transportation and length of time on the fire line. The metaphors provide a semantic arena in which these differences can be manipulated and dealt with while the occupational goals and techniques remain basically the same.

To provide a specific example, the following narrative is taken from a tape I recorded with some jumpers in 1969 and it illustrates in some detail the importance of the relationship between jumpers and ground crew members. The speaker is an experienced squad leader who at the time of the recording had been a jumper for over twenty-five years:

Speaking of glorious, I'll tell you a story—it's got kind of dirty strip here, I guess. In '55 after I got back from Silver City, I jumped on a fire in the Lumberg District, up Ingles—no Icicle? Along Icicle Ridge, anyway. It was one of those hairy goddamn things, you know, where the wind'd blow across the shittin' ridge. The side that we got off on was vertical cliff for about two thousand feet down into the

Tumwater Canyon. The side wasn't too bad; it sloped off fast and old Gus dropped us on the bottom of the cliff. And I was ready to get out long before we decided we were going to go. Fortunately he was right, or I'd have been way in the hell down over the other side. But anyway we went down to that fire. And there were four of us on it. And it wasn't a tough fire. It was—parts—of bits and pieces were tough, you know. You'd have a flare up in the brush and one thing or another. We pretty much had it. The district sent in two guys. And they knew jumpers was running the fire so didn't send in any tools or sleeping bags. They come in, for all practical purposes, empty. Well, as it turned out, when they dropped the cargo, they waited for us to get down to the fire before they dropped the cargo, because we were up on the top of the ridge and the fire was halfway down. So, we got down there and they dropped the cargo. Well, all we saw was two runs. And in those days the chow and the water were packaged individually. You got four fire packs and two chow packs for four guys and then the water packs for four guys. So all told, you had a whole bunch of parachutes. We ended up with four fire packs, the jumpers' rations and two jumpers' water, which left us with just exactly enough for what we supposedly needed for two days. That wasn't a problem until they put two district guys in there that didn't have diddley shit with them anyway, you know. So here's six guys going to live on—what it amounts to, about four o'clock the next morning we were just flat out of groceries and we were out of water.

Turned out we found some water but it involved walking about a mile and a half around the ridge to get it. And well, we were on the fire the first day from about noon on and then the next day and all day. And then they brought in—what was the name of the guard station over on the other side of Bullett Pass? Used to have a suppression crew—it doesn't make a damn anyway. They used to have a little twelve man suppression crew at this place. So they brought them in there and those guys had all belt canteens on them. And they come in, what was it, a day like the third morning of the fire. And they wouldn't give us any water. So that pissed us off, see. The four of us, six of us. Of course the two guys that came in, one of them I knew real well. I'd gone to college with him. And it really pissed us off that these guys wouldn't give us any water. So shortly after that, about ten o'clock that morning we got a water drop, two five gallon cans from a Super Cub. They're wind-loaded para-containers you can mount over each wing and kick it loose and the chute would come up to two five gallon cans of water. One hung way in the hell up in a shittin' tree. One landed on the ground. Well as it turned out about that time the suppresive crew foreman turned up and wanted to have some water, see. We said there's your water right up there about sixty feet. And we picked our can up and wandered off.[5]

Embedded in this jump story is a detailed personal presentation of the relationship between jumpers and ground crewmen described above. The jumpers, although independent on a jump, are also more vulnerable because of their reliance on air support for food and water; while the ground crew is usually from the area and more familiar with what to expect and how to provision themselves. The loss of the two water packs on the initial drop left the jumpers in a much more vulnerable position that required them to seek aid from the ground crew. The refusal of the crew to cooperate and the eventual victory of the jumpers creates a vivid and lasting image of anger and frustration turned to what the jumpers would see as justified revenge. Beyond supporting and backing up the metaphorical contention between these two groups, this jump story would be particularly convincing and entertaining to other jumpers because it is based on an extremely tight narration of a fire jump that fulfills the expectations of the audience. The names of specific locations, nature and character of the fire, loss of water packs and particularly the refusal of ground crewmen to provide the most importance substance on a fire—water—provides irrevocable proof supporting the jumpers' stereotypes of the ground crew by extracting out of the actual experience key images and symbols of particular importance to this audience. This suggests that the creation of key occupational metaphors may be on the narrative level when members of the occupational group feature selected aspects of the work experience in their verbal accounts and as these features are repeated they begin to assume greater metaphorical importance and independence.

The media, in their designation of the jumpers as "commandoes" and the ground crew as "legions" or the "fire fighting infantry," maintain a parallel metaphorical relationship between the more individualistic jumpers and the more regimented ground crew, while placing further semantic distance between the occupational experience and the written pictorial account by maintaining a consistent military metaphor.[6] We can trace the development of these terms from the actual work experience (jumping/ground crew suppression) to internally derived designations (hot dogs/pounders), which in turn suggest an externally maintained metaphor (commandoes/infantry). The media account attempts to create a literary frame of reference around the work and relationship of the two groups, while the original terms are based on specific collective behaviors and used daily as pronouns. Both sets of terms shape and are shaped by a perception of work techniques: the internally derived metaphor by operating as a rhetorical means of identification, accommodation and movement within two functionally similar but contentious groups of workers, and the media designation by maintaining a literary analogy of the military to establish a referent upon which outsiders can grasp the relationship between the two groups. The popular presentation is not wrong, it is just partially right and it is the looseness yet partial accuracy of the media employed metaphors that continually reinforces our occupational stereotypes.

When we watch "Hill Street Blues" or "The Jeffersons," for example, we encounter characters who are portrayed against an occupational backdrop which is filled with these loose metaphors. It is difficult, however, to determine the effects of these metaphorical backgrounds and the stereotypes they generate. Similar characters in shows like "Alice" perpetuate a class stereotype based almost exclusively on the improper use of standard English, specifically through the use of elaborated malapropisms. This caricature of the working-class speaker and our association of this metaphorical characterization with monosyllables— beer drinking—and physical violence was epitomized in the media's coverage of the hard hat/student confrontations in New York City and Chicago during the sixties as well as perpetuated in films like "Flash Dance" and "The Flamingo Kid."

The presentation of blacks and women in occupational settings has also been subjected to similar selectively chosen metaphors which are often complicated by ethnic or sexual stereotypes as well. Television programs like "The Jeffersons" and "Sanford and Son" depict black small-business- men as borderline incompetents, and black entrepreneurship as a continual process of frustrated greed; whereas programs like "Remington Steele" and "Alice" rarely attempt to transcend the sexual and romantic aspects of the occupational experience to deal with substantive aspects of these women's actual work.

Putting aside artistic licence and the need to create an engaging character, these fuzzy and often blatantly discriminatory and misleading "loose" occupational metaphors may appear innocuous enough because of the vague background nature of most of the occupational frameworks and their submersion under strong characterization. But the work of Joseph Wambaugh presenting the police as the "new centurions" on both television and in films, the AMA's endorsement of Dr. Welby, M.D. and the FBI's endorsement of a TV program representing the work of its officers, suggests that at least these organizations considered the depictions presented worthy of comment. We have seen the policeman's popular occupational stereotype evolve from the whistling Irishman twirling his billy on the street corner through the "Fascist Pig" designation of the sixties to the SWAT team assassinating a sniper with complete military precision of today. None of these images have the ethnographic integrity of a study like that done by Jonathan Rubinstein on the Philadelphia Police Department, but they all draw metaphorically significant key skills and behaviors which provide them with enough credibility to both reflect a portion of the occupational reality and possibly shape our expectations toward workers in this trade.[7]

The internal impact of key metaphorical skills and stereotypes in an occupation is much more difficult to document, but I do have an illustration taken from my fieldwork. Several years ago while doing fieldwork with urban fire fighters in Washington, D.C., we were all sitting in the dining room of the station house watching television. "Emergency" was on and the fire fighters were not only picking out the stiffness of acting and the lack of accuracy in the depicted fire, but were using the incidents of the dramatized scene to make jokes and comments about their own actual performances on the fire ground earlier that day. When I asked them about the accuracy of media presentations in general and specifically the portrayal of their work in "Emergency" they unanimously expressed approval of the show because, as they said, it made fire fighters look professional while it also helped to "destroy the myth that all fire fighters do is sit around, sleep all day and play checkers."

There are two significant concepts in this incident that suggest the importance of popular presentations of occupational culture. First, many of the actual work techniques which were presented during the program were rejected as being impossible to do in the first place, done wrong or impossible to show, while at the same time these activities were close enough to the real thing to suggest topics of personal experience narratives resulting from actual fire ground experiences. Secondly, the sensitivity of the fire fighters to accusations about laziness, sitting around all day and just playing checkers is (from the fire fighters' point of view) countered by "Emergency's" continual presentation of fire fighters who just return to the station in time to have a quick cup of coffee and then rush off to deal with another catastrophe.

Both the internal use of dramatized action as a precipitant to narrative and the approval of the attack against a popular myth are an indication of this occupational groups' acceptance of the key skills which have metaphorically been extracted to represent the work done by urban fire fighters; basically because the stereotype is flattering. At the same time, however, the discrepancy between the actual occupational experience on a fire or in a rescue and the television presentation requires critical comment. This comment takes the form of personal experience narratives which are employed (perhaps) to rhetorically move the TV presentation closer to a view of the occupation that is consistent with the internal perspective. The rhetorical strategy of using a narrative to qualify and evaluate a TV drama reverses the media's metaphorical movement away from experience by personalizing it and restating it in a way that is acceptable to the specific work group; while at the same time it condones the public metaphor and resulting stereotype because it is flattering and addresses itself to an area which they feel the public does not properly understand—why fire fighters are allowed to sit around and even sleep on the job.

Whether the need for critical comment is precipitated by internal or external metaphors or activities, the result is a verbal response that may be the basis of occupational folklore. Both the media and the internally derived metaphors are based on work experience—the former is just loose and abstract while the latter is tighter and situation specific. The folklore of the workplace might therefore be conceived of as that collective body of critical comment and behavior which concerns itself with experiences and metaphors linked to a certain type of work.

I have attempted in this discussion to illustrate the way in which we as workers and members of the popular audience create and are influenced by metaphors based on key occupational techniques and experiences. These metaphors provide us with the ability to gain an understanding of other people's work by translating it into a category or domain which has meaning to us. When we accept the inaccurately presented or extracted metaphor we perpetuate a certain type of expectation or belief which we may or may not consider an appropriate public image. Yet this strategic use of metaphors takes place on a number of different levels of meaning at once in both the public and private occupational context and therefore the only realistic way to understand its use is through the "thick description" of a thinly sliced segment of the occupational pie.[8] To arbitrarily isolate any one aspect of expressive behavior over another is a prejudgement of the actual ethnographic situation that imposes yet another "loose" metaphor between us and our attempt to describe things as the insider experienced them.

Notes

[1]F.C. Bartlett, "The Measurement of Human Skill," *Occupational Psychology*, 22:1 and 2 (1948), 31-39, 83-92.

[2]Donald Roy, "Banana Time: Job Satisfaction and Informal Interaction," *Human Organization*, 18 (1960), 158-160; Eli Chinoy, *Automobile Workers and the American Dream* (Garden City, N.Y.: Doubleday, 1955); Robert Blauner, *Alienation and Freedom: The Factory Worker and His Industry* (Chicago: Univ. of Chicago Press, 1964).

[3]James Fernandez, "Persuasions and Performances: Of the Beast in Every Body ... And the Metaphors of Everyman," in Clifford Geertz, ed., *Myth, Symbol and Culture* (New York: Norton, 1971), p. 57.

[4]*Ibid.*, p. 47.

[5]Robert McCarl, Smokejumper Folklore, tape and transcript collection housed in the Randall Mills Folklore Archive, Univ. of Oregon, 1969, 37-39.

[6]Stuart E. Jones and Jay Johnston, "Forest Fire: The Devil's Picnic," *National Geographic*, 134:1 (July 1968), 108-110.

[7]Jonathan Rubinstein, *City Police* (New York: Farrar, Strauss & Giroux, 1973).

[8]Clifford Geertz, "Thick Description: Toward an Interpretive Theory of Culture," in Clifford Geertz, ed., *The Interpretation of Cultures* (New York: Basic Books, 1973), pp. 3-33.

Holy Pictures in Newfoundland Houses: Visual Codes for Secular and Supernatural Relationships

Gerald L. Pocius

ALTHOUGH FOLKLORISTS have researched mass-produced forms of verbal genres, little investigation has been conducted on artifacts that are the products of popular culture.[1] Part of this reluctance stems from a largely rural emphasis in previous folkloristic investigation of objects; the study of traditional "crafts" has almost become synonymous with the study of material culture within the discipline. This lack of research on popular culture artifacts is also related to the implicit designation of folk artifacts as those that are homemade, thus making the defining criteria the mode of production. With this approach, the initial act of creation becomes all important, and the subsequent function is of little importance in determining which objects can be studied.[2] Yet, objects—whatever their mode of production—can follow specific traditional rules of use that are manifested in various behaviors such as spatial organization. How an object is used following these rules may become more important for the folklorist than how it was actually made. Material objects are just one of the subsystems of the entire cultural complex, and provide insight into cultural values that often are more difficult to interpret by focusing on other forms of behavior.[3] All of us are surrounded by mass-produced objects of every description, yet little is known of how different individuals organize their daily lives through these artifacts. Such is the case with the objects we place in our homes.[4]

In many cultures, the walls of a dwelling do not merely act as a means of dividing space into specific functional areas. They are often used as vehicles of display, providing the frame in which visual objects can be placed that communicate some type of message about the room and its uses. The entire visual environment thus becomes a code that is concerned with specific types of behavior. As Kevin Lynch has recently written:

Like law and custom, environment tells us how to act without requiring of us a conscious choice. In a church we are reverent and on a beach relaxed. Much of the time, we are reenacting patterns of behaviour associated with particular recognizable settings.[5]

Settings are recognizable partly through the objects they contain, with wall decorations forming one important unit of this behavioral code. Erving Goffman posits that one person utilizes various methods of presenting different faces of him or herself;[6] so too can the occupants of a house present different facets of its life to both family members and visitors by placing the culturally accepted images on the walls which speak to these specific spatial domains. This essay will deal with one aspect of this visual dimension found in particular Roman Catholic homes in Newfoundland.

One of the major concerns of daily life is the relationship of the human being to the supernatural, and most Newfoundland houses until recently had a number of religious prints dealing with public and private devotional figures. From the mid-nineteenth century, when popular, mass-produced prints dealing with secular as well as sacred objects began to be hung on the walls of the common dwelling house throughout North America,[7] "holy pictures"—as they are often referred to in Newfoundland—have been common in the island's homes. Only in the last twenty years has their use begun to decline.

Devotional prints were common both in Roman Catholic and Protestant homes in Newfoundland. Although this essay will concern itself with the popular prints found in the Roman Catholic home, a thematically different but equally vigorous tradition existed in Protestant homes.[8] The conclusions of this particular study are based on approximately one hundred examples of Roman Catholic devotional prints examined to date, fifty in two Irish Roman Catholic areas of the island: the Southern Shore and the Cape Shore, both on the Avalon Peninsula south of St. John's. This initial investigation will point to the origins and types of popular religious prints found in the home, but more importantly will discuss how these images metaphorically reveal attitudes toward personal interrelationships on both spiritual and secular levels.

The ultimate origins of many religious prints used in the Newfoundland home are often difficult to determine. Most holy pictures have no specific marking that indicates where they were printed; however, the title of most is found at the bottom, usually printed in five languages: French, Spanish, English, German and Italian. From this it is obvious that these prints were geared toward a worldwide market, perhaps the entire European and North American Roman Catholic community. Generally, most of these prints seem to have been manufactured in Europe. One likeness of St. Louisa, for example, specifies that it was printed in Germany, while versions of the Sacred Heart of Jesus and Mater Dolorosa contain ecclesiastical approval from the diocese of Limbourg in Belgium.

To date, seven prints that have been located actually contain the name of a printer and place of manufacture (Table 1). Of these, six are mid-nineteenth century lithographs, technologically similar to prints utilizing this printing process found in other areas of the world. The outline of the entire image has been printed—often poorly—in black, and any desired color was added later at the printers by hand (figure 1). Only a version of the Crucifixion entitled "Jesus Dies" provides a signed example of the later, more common printing process whereby both color and outline are printed to provide more complex color schemes. The Belgian and German prints previously mentioned also exhibit this process, and there may have been a gradual shift by the twentieth century in the ultimate origins of popular religious prints found in Newfoundland from Paris to other regions of Europe. Throughout this time period, the United States continued to supply religious images for popular consumption.

Table 1
Printers of Newfoundland Roman Catholice Religious Prints

Print Title	Printer
Jesus Dies	James Lee, Chicago, Ill.
Ecce Homo	J. Lechevallier, 109 Broadway, New York City
Notre Dame de la Garde	Bes, Paris (sold by Dubreuil, Paris)
Our Lady of Lourdes	Haskell and Allen, 61 Hanover St., Boston, Mass.
Sacre Coeur de Jesus	Vayron, Paris (sold by Condoni, Paris)
Sacred Heart of Jesus	Currier and Ives, 125 Nassau St., New York
Madona aux Pervenches	Pierre Langlade, Paris, chez DAZIARO, 15 Boul. des Italiens

The actual distribution of these prints in Newfoundland followed both official and unofficial channels. Many reports exist of door-to-door peddlers selling large numbers of religious prints, and one woman on the Southern Shore related that one or two holy pictures were often bought simply to get rid of the travelling salesperson. Another woman from the same area claimed that these salespeople were often thought to have come from "Arab countries like Lebanon," and since these regions were considered part of the Holy Land, there was no surprise that darker-skinned strangers would sell such prints. Although the assumed special origins of peddlers often made their product more desirable, there has also been a tradition in Newfoundland of non-English or non-Irish acting as travelling salespeople, and in many cases what would be an ethnic and racial outsider would have his or her wares purchased because of the potential for magical harm if this were not done.[9]

Besides these secular channels, church organizations promoted the sale and distribution of popular prints. Local priests distributed holy pictures in their parishes, making them available either through sale or providing them as gifts. Father J.A. Miller, parish priest at St. Bride's on the Cape Shore in the early twentieth century, for example, gave prints of St. Theresa of the Little Flower to parishioners as a Christmas and New Years gift. These prints had "Wishing you a Merry Christmas and a Prosperous New Year" embossed on the top left corner, as well as Father Miller's name, and the company selling these prints obviously had such uses in mind by providing the option of this additional lettering.

The Redemptorist Priests, one of the first groups of missionaries to come to Newfoundland, also were instrumental in distributing various types of holy pictures. Before permanent priests were stationed in outport communities—often not until the mid-nineteenth century—missionaries would distribute both devotional books and images to those they visited.[10] Even after the establishment of permanent parishes with resident clergy, the Redemptorist Order conducted parish missions throughout the island, and at these missions, which generally consisted of a week of services and devotions conducted by these visiting clergy, numerous prints were distributed.[11] Images of holy personages to which the Order had a special devotion, such as Our Lady of Perpetual Help (Figure 2), were distributed at these week-long missions, a practice followed by Redemptorist missionaries in other areas of the world.[12]

Popular religious publications also added to the wide distribution of these materials, usually containing ads for religious prints that could be ordered through the mail. *The Eikon* and *Madonna*, both published by the Redemptorists, often had advertisements for such prints accompanied by explanations of the spiritual benefits of having such images in the home.[13] Catholic newspapers played a similar role in distribution; one framed print of Our Lady of the Rosary used in Newfoundland was backed with the front page of *The Catholic Record*, a newspaper published in London, Ontario; the page was dated November 24, 1917. The owner of this print subscribed to *The Catholic Record* by mail, and although this front page does not specifically mention holy pictures, it is likely that newspapers of this type contributed to the spread of these images—as well as providing convenient backing material.

The subjects depicted in the devotional prints can be grouped into four major categories (Table 2): those dealing with Christ; Mary; the saints; contemporary religious leaders and buildings. Perhaps the most singularly widespread topic of all religious prints—as well as being the most popular depiction of Christ—was the image of the Sacred Heart of Jesus. Often referred to in earlier prints as "The Holy Heart," this image of

Figure 1. A mid-nineteenth century lithograph of the Sacred Heart of Jesus, printed in Paris. From a house in Renews.

Figure 2. Our Lady of Perpetual Help, a devotion spread by the Redemptorist Order. From a house in St. John's.

Christ was common in both the earlier mid-nineteenth century types (figure 1), as well as the later versions (figure 3). As Yvonne Lange points out, this image does not appear in iconography until the seventeenth century with the apparition of Christ to St. Margaret Mary Alacoque.[14] Perhaps one of the reasons for its widespread popularity as a religious print in many areas of the world including Newfoundland was Christ's promise to St. Margaret Mary for blessings on those who not only prayed to the Sacred Heart but actually displayed this image in public. A recent comment on this practice points to the sentiments that have led to its popularity:

> Jesus wishes to rule the Christian family by means of the devotion to His Sacred Heart. Our Lord promised that He would bless abundantly every place where the picture of His Loving Heart would be exposed for veneration and love. He will unite disrupted divorced families, protect others from great disasters, pour forth His burning love on all families, homes, and businesses, where the picture of His Sacred Heart is honored. It is our Savior's wish then, that the picture of His Sacred Heart be exposed publicly, not merely kept in a book.[15]

TABLE 2

SUBJECT MATTER OF NEWFOUNDLAND
ROMAN CATHOLIC RELIGIOUS PRINTS

Christ	Saints
Holy Grave of Christ	St. Louisa
Christ Carrying His Cross	St. Cecilia
Holy or Sacred Heart of Jesus	St. Theresa
Ecce Homo	St. Anthony
Jesus Dies	St. Joseph

Mary	Earthly Church
Holy Grave of Mary	Pope Pius XI
Our Lady of the Rosary	Pope Leo XIII
Our Lady of Lourdes	Basilica of St. John the Baptist, St. John's
Notre Dame de la Garde	
Our Lady of Mount Carmel	
Holy Heart of Mary	
Our Lady of Guadalupe	
Our Lady of the Most Blessed Sacrament	
Madona aux Pervenches	

A more recent devotion has also contributed to the widespread distribution of this image. Since around 1915, families have been encouraged to "enthrone" the Sacred Heart in their home, dedicating the house and family to the Sacred Heart and displaying his image in a prominent place. As Raymond Firth points out, "What it means is a dedication to a way of life in which love is fostered by the sharing of family interests with Christ and Mary by frequent renewal of the consecration to the Sacred Union in union with the Immaculate Heart of Mary, and by a fuller liturgical life at home and in church."[16] A typical image of the Sacred Heart often has a section under it that contains the dedication prayer, and a place where the members of the family can write their names. A dedication from Calvert on the Southern Shore, dated June 24, 1938, contains one of the standard forms.

Figure 3. One of the many later versions of the Sacred Heart of Jesus.

Consecration of the Family to the Sacred Heart

We consecrate to thee, O Jesus of love, the trials and joys and all the happiness of our family life, and we beseech thee to pour out thy blessings on all its members, absent and present, living and dead—and when one after the other, we shall have fallen asleep in Thy blessed bosom, O Jesus, may all of us in Paradise find again our family united in Thy Sacred Heart. Amen.

This ....day of .... 19.....
           Signed, ...

Part of the devotion to the Sacred Heart consisted of night prayers and adoration, and in the past most houses kept a red votive candle burning beneath this image throughout the night in response to this aspect of worship. Today, seven and one-half watt red light bulbs have often replaced the votive light, and they are still kept lit all night. During a drive through a community late at night the faint red glow of the Sacred Heart light can often be seen in the kitchen window of the darkened house.

Unlike the image of the Sacred Heart, the other depictions of Christ center almost exclusively on his passion and death. Scenes of Christ carrying his cross as the women of Jerusalem weep over him, the actual crucifixion, and a print entitled "Ecce Homo" (Figure 4) are common. The latter picture contains a view of Christ's anguished face after his scourging. One version contains two drops of blood dripping down the right side of Christ's neck, and one resident of Branch on the Cape Shore mentioned that everyone looking at this print would always be initially struck by these two drops.

Besides these views, a print entitled in English "Holy Grave of Christ," but in French as "Sepulcher of Christ in Jerusalem," contains the body of Christ inside what appears to be a cave, flanked by angels on either side (Figure 5). In front of the body lies the cross and instruments of the passion, while behind it is an altar with candles and the Eucharistic host and chalice. Above the altar hover four cherub heads. This scene hung over the bed of one woman in Calvert when she was young, and she remembered that she and her sisters were always afraid to get out of bed at night out of fear of these angel heads—the "fuzzy things" as they always called them.

The images of Mary show her role as various patrons. The "Holy Heart of Mary," usually referred to today as the Immaculate Heart, parallels visually the Sacred Heart image, although in terms of devotion there is much less intensity. One mid-nineteenth century print (Figure 6) found in Renews on the Southern Shore entitled "Notre Dame de la Garde" was published in Paris and shows the figure of Mary holding the Christ Child in her arms. The right section of the print shows three ships in

Figure 4. A print entitled "Ecco Homo." From a house in Branch.

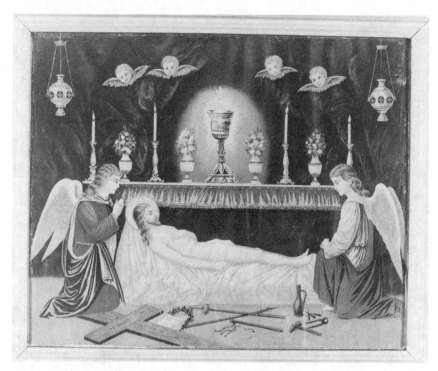

Figure 5. "The Holy Grave of Christ."

a harbor, one flying the French tri-color. The print of "Our Lady of the Rosary" (Figure 7) shows Mary again holding the Christ Child, in this scene with a rosary in his hands. Bordering Mary and the child are scenes of what are known as the "Mysteries of the Rosary"; these fifteen events comprise the five joyful, five sorrowful and five glorious mysteries.[17] Each mystery depicts a scene in the life of Christ or Mary which should be meditated upon when that particular section of the rosary is recited. The image of the "Mater Dolorosa"—Mother of Sorrows—is a counterpart of the "Ecce Homo" image of Christ, and shows a sorrowful face of Mary.

In iconography, the image of Mary as "Our Lady of Mount Carmel" often depicts her interceding for the souls in purgatory.[18] In a Newfoundland version recorded on the Southern Shore (Figure 8), she is shown holding the Christ Child with several scapulars in his hands. One woman remembered that she was always told as a child that this image indicated that it was important to wear a scapular, since it was believed that if you died wearing it and went to purgatory, the flames would burn only so high as the scapular.

Like the "Holy Grave of Christ," a similar print exists of the "Holy Grave of Mary" (Figure 9), and they seem to form almost a matching set. Like the print of Christ, the body of Mary is flanked by two angels, one

Figure 6. Notre Dame de la Garde, printed in Paris, from a house in Renews. Note the ship to the right flying the French tri-color.

Figure 7. Our Lady of the Rosary, from a house in Branch. Mary and the Christ Child are surrounded by the Mysteries of the Rosary.

Figure 8. "Our Lady of Mount Carmel," from a house in Calvert. Mary and the Christ Child intercede for the souls in purgatory.

Figure 9. "The Holy Grave of Mary."

with a palm branch, the other with an incense thurible or censer. In front of the body lies a cushion holding a crown; beside it lies a rosary book, sword and a crown of thorns. Behind the body is an altar with candles and a vase containing lillies. Overhead flutter the same four cherubim as in the print of Christ. This print is remarkable for its apocryphal content, since little is mentioned in scripture of the death of Mary.

All the images of the saints are quite standard iconographic depictions. St. Joseph, for example, holds the Chirst Child and the staff that flowered, the most widespread image of this saint (Figure 10).[19] St. Cecilia, patroness of music, plays an organ while flowers descend from heaven.[20] Besides images of saints, prints of what would be contemporary religious leaders, or views of famous churches are widespread. Popes and bishops are the most common personages, while prominent Newfoundland churches, such as the Basilica of St. John the Baptist in St. John's, are the most numerous among views of ecclesiastical buildings.

Like many approaches to the study of individual items, the holy pictures found in the Newfoundland home could be examined strictly as discrete objects that follow particular patterns with regard to distribution and content. However, these images function within the specified cultural context of the home, and are one part of the visual environment that

Figure 10. "St. Joseph with the Christ Child," from a house in Branch. This print is captioned in German, Italian, English and Spanish.

Figure 11. The common front room photograph of the family's ancestors, taken around the turn of the century. From a house in Calvert.

influences, and in turn is influenced by, specific behavioral codes. The content and placement of these prints can only be understood by considering them as part of a complete spatial system, whereby objects placed within certain behavioral domains are indicative of the relationships and action that take place within those spaces.

To understand the use of holy pictures within the Newfoundland home, it is necessary to be aware of the general spatial configuration of the typical house. Until recently the vast majority of houses contained three major spatial domains: the kitchen, the front room or parlor, and the bedrooms. Most houses were two stories, and contained a central hallway on both floors. Each of these major spatial domains contained specific patterns of social interaction.

The kitchen of the house was the room to which all members of the community had free access. The outside door was never locked, and neighbors and friends walked in and out at will, often during the visits of others. Even today the constant interaction in the kitchen can often be bewildering to the outsider, for announcements of arrival or departure are sometimes not used, and several conversations often take place concurrently. Like the hall in the medieval European house, most of the day-to-day living has taken place in this room.

On the other hand, the front room has been the special room of the house. It was rarely used, generally only for strangers or honored guests such as the clergyman. This room was often kept locked, and in several respects was a nonfunctional space that would be used only a few times a year. The finest of the family's possessions would be placed in this room, potentially to be displayed to the outsider.

The bedroom area was the most private space in the home, and would be used almost exclusively for sleeping. Often several family members would share a room, sometimes three or four children to a bed. Even members of the same community would rarely see the bedrooms of other houses; instead, any visit would be centered in the kitchen. When I asked one man in Calvert about the floor plan of a house in the community that was now demolished, he responded that he really could not comment about it, since he had been only "in the kitchen part" of the house during his many visits.

The themes of the religious prints found in the Newfoundland home act as visual metaphors for the types of secular and supernatural relationships which are expected to take place in each spatial domain.[21] In the kitchen are hung those religious images which are concerned basically with what are widespread community religious devotions. Primarily this is an image of the Sacred Heart—often with a Consecration. The dedication of the house and family to the Sacred Heart reassures the community visitor of the faith of his or her neighbor; as well, it is a constant reminder to the members of the household of their devotion as such a unit. Even the faint glow of the Sacred Heart light at night in a community is a reminder to others of this widespread belief and subsequent protection.

In the bedrooms the images of personal religious devotion are found. Practically all the holy pictures used in the home have been found in the bedrooms. The images of Christ suffering, the various icons of Mary, and the numerous views of the saints are all are placed in this spatial domain. Each morning and evening devotional prayers to special figures could be said. This is especially the case with the images of Mary and the various saints, for these figures were often chosen because of individual needs and petitions. If Mary and the saints are mediational figures between the natural and the supernatural,[22] they carry out this role on an individual basis and in the most private of spaces in the home.

The concern with the death of Christ and, to a lesser extent, the death of Mary, in images found in the bedroom speaks of the didactic values of these artifacts. Many prints stressed the importance of suffering and death, both having to be expected and accepted. As the images depicted Christ accepting suffering and pain, so too must the individual in his or her daily life.[23] And as Christ accepted death, so must the individual. As one writer in a Redemptorist publication stated:

The longer our trials the longer must we remain beneath the Cross of Christ; the heavier they are, the closer must we draw to it; the harder they are to bear, the more earnestly must we gaze up into the face of the Crucified. We must look lovingly upon those precious wounds "poor dumb mouths" which will "open their ruby lips" to teach us the heavenly wisdom of love of the Cross.[24]

The presence of images in the bedroom dealing with death is not surprising, given the fact that until recently most individuals in a Newfoundland home expected to die in this room, and that death could often come unexpectedly during sleep. These images reminded the occupant of the ever-present possibility of death, and the necessity of its acceptance. Perhaps the most telling example of this connection between death and the spatial domain of the bedroom was the fact that years ago the roof of one particular house on the Southern Shore was raised to add upstairs bedrooms because the owner wanted to die in the area of the house considered the locus for death.

In general, the front room has been relegated to the secular realm, and to interactions with outsiders, and few if any devotional pictures are found in this room. Those connected with religion are generally images of leaders of the church, such as popes or bishops, or scenes of religious buildings. In a sense, these are closer to images of secular leaders, and have minimal connection to daily religious devotions. Instead of sacred themes, this room is devoted to secular concerns of family history; the temporal dimension produced by these images[25] also provides a sense of the collective family self.[26] Ancestral photographs of parents or grandparents are found here (Figure 11), as well as images preserving and proclaiming the rites of passage of family members. Wedding photographs, kindergarten graduation pictures, and pubescent competition awards— the hockey and dart trophies—are all found there. In this room where strangers of perhaps unknown religious denominations would be brought, no overt statements of religious belief were made by the family.

Besides these three major spatial domains that contain prints which speak of specific conceptual usages, some devotional images are found connected to other features, such as the doorway or the hall. Many studies have been conducted on the notion of doorway as threshold which can ambiguously bring either good or bad through it,[27] and many cultures fix various artifacts over the doorway to ensure the safety of a room. The Newfoundland house is no different, and religious images are usually found over particular entrances. Probably the most common item is a small stamped metal cross—formerly made of paper—depicting the Sacred Heart (Figure 12), with the inscription: "I will bless the house in which the picture of my Sacred Heart shall be exposed." These are often placed over the kitchen doorway where visitors would enter; some have been there for so many years that they have been covered with layers of paint and are hardly legible.

One other spatial domain must be mentioned in terms of religious images, an area containing both prints and statues. At the top of the stairs of many homes on the Southern Shore and Cape Shore, a small table or shelf fastened to the wall is used as a family altar (Figure 13).[28] This upstairs hallway would be the only area of the house used by all members of the family but not in view of the normal visitor. It would be directly in view as one climbed the stairs, and would be passed coming to and from the bedrooms in the morning and evening. This altar contains images and statues of various patron saints that have played important roles in the religious lives of the family. This altar often is decorated during certain months of the year, as in May, a month dedicated to the veneration of Mary, and special prayers are often said at it. If this area of the house can be considered by the family as one of the few strictly private spaces, then devotional images concerning the family are placed there.

The religious images, from the Sacred Heart to the saints, from the Holy Grave of Christ to the Souls in Purgatory, become visual reminders of

Figure 12. A Sacred Heart medal over the kitchen door of a house in Calvert.

Figure 13. The family altar, common in houses on the Cape Shore and the Southern Shore, usually located in the upstairs hallway. From a house in Calvert.

the spiritual and secular relationships that transpire in specific spatial domains within the house. The day-to-day social relationships that occur within the home become behavioral dimensions of the more visual metaphors found on the walls. As J.W. Fernandez points out in his study of the importance of metaphor in culture, men know and understand their experiences—in this case the Newfoundlander's relationships with others—by referring them to other domains for elucidation.[29] The attitude toward the community generally is referred to in the beliefs shared by the community of believers in terms of common devotions. And likewise, as salvation is the ultimate concern of the individual—with the potential help of individual patron saints—this spatial domain of the bedroom is kept personal. The devotional prints found on the walls of the Newfoundland house do not mirror the expected social relationships common to the home; rather, both the visual objects and the behavioral activities are part of a more fundamental concern with the ordering of daily cultural space. In this ordering, in fact, the sacred and the secular become integrated into acceptable domains, making the separation of sacred and profane less marked. By integrating both levels, day-to-day relationships both with fellow humans and with supernatural figures become regulated by the same concerns. These popular prints, then, while created by the thousands in far-removed lands, become visual signs in the Newfoundland home of the very personal belief that the two great commandments of Christ could be followed on a daily basis more practically as one. To a great extent, then, the same behavioral rules governed both neighbor and God.

Notes

[1]Versions of this essay were presented at the Folklore Studies Association of Canada meeting, London, Ontario, June, 1978, and the American Folklore Society meeting, Los Angeles, California, Oct. 1979. I would like to thank Ronald Labelle and Mac Swackhammer for comments during various stages of this paper; special thanks are given to Walter Peddle whose enthusiasm and assistance have made much of this study possible. This study is a revised version of an essay that originally appeared in *Laurentian University Review*, 12:1 (1979).

[2]For comments on the issue of defining folk objects by creation or function see Henry Glassie, *Pattern in the Material Folk Culture of the Eastern United States*, University of Pennsylvania Publications in Folklore and Folklife 1 (Philadelphia: Univ. of Pennsylvania Press, 1968), pp. 11-15; on the reasons why folklorists have neglected the study of certain types of objects see Gerald L. Pocius, "Beyond Arts and Crafts: Past Paradigms and Future Directions in Folkloristic Material Culture Studies," paper read at the Folklore Studies Association of Canada Meeting, Montreal, Quebec, June, 1980; for a recent study of artifacts influenced by popular culture see Michael Owen Jones, "L.A. Add-ons and Re-dos: Renovation in Folk Art and Architectural Design," in Ian M.G. Quimby and Scott T. Swank, eds., *Perspectives on American Folk Art* (New York: Norton, for Winterthur Museum, 1980), pp. 325-63.

[3]For the relationship of material objects to other cultural subsystems see David L. Clarke, *Analytical Archeology* (2nd ed. New York: Columbia Univ. Press, 1978), pp. 84-148.

[4]The study of house interiors as cultural systems has been largely neglected; a few exceptions are, Jean E. Hess, "Domestic Interiors in Rural New Mexico," paper read at the American Folklore Society meeting, Los Angeles, California, Oct., 1979; John Collier, Jr., *Visual Anthropology: Photography as a Research Method* (New York: Holt, Rinehart and Winston, 1967), pp. 77-104; John M. Roberts, *Three Navaho Households: A Comparative Study of Small Group Culture*, Peabody Museum Papers, 40:3 (Cambridge: Harvard Univ. Press, 1951); Judith Hansen, "The Proxemics of Danish Daily Life," *Studies in the Anthropology of Visual Communication*, 3 (1976), 52-62; J.W. Fernandez, *Fang Architectonics*, Working Papers in the Traditional Arts (Philadelphia: Institute for the Study of Human Issues, 1976), pp. 13-22; Frank M. Le Bar, "A Household Survey of Economic Goods on Romonum Island, Truk," in Ward H. Goodenough, ed. *Explorations in Cultural Anthropology: Essays in Honor of George Peter Murdock* (New York: McGraw-Hill, 1964), pp. 335-49.

[5]Kevin Lynch, *What Time Is This Place?* (Cambridge and London: MIT Press, 1972), p. 40; for other comments on this point see Amos Rapoport, "Environment and People," in his *Australia as Human Setting* (Sydney: Angus and Robertson, 1972), p. 15; Roland Barthes, *Mythologies*, trans. Annette Lavers (New York: Hill and Wang, 1972), p. 110; Amos Rapoport, "The Ecology of Housing," *Ecologist*, 3 (1973), 12.

[6]Erving Goffman, *The Presentation of Self in Everyday Life* (Garden City: Doubleday/Anchor, 1959).

[7]See Russell Lynes, *The Taste-Makers* (New York: Harper and Bros., 1954), pp. 65-80 for one of the few discussions of early mass-produced prints in North America. In contrast, much research has been conducted on popular prints in Europe; for example see Jean Adhemar, *Populare Druckgraphik Europas: Frankreich vom 15. bis zum 20. Jahrhundert* (Munchen:

Verlag Georg D.W. Callwey, 1968); Wolfgang Brucker, *Populare Druckgraphik Europas: Deutschland vom 15. bis zum 20. Jahrhundert* (Munchen: Verlag D.W. Callwey, 1969); Jean Mistler, Francois Blaudez and Andre Jacquemin, *Epinal et l'imagerie populaire* (N.P.: Hachette, 1961).

[8]Protestant popular prints seem to have stressed Biblical scenes and those containing angels guiding humans. For an example of two typical prints see *Goldenseal*, 5:3 (July-September, 1979), 70.

[9]Peggy Martin points out that many Micmac Indians were assured sales of their baskets in outport communities through the belief that they could bring harm to those who did not buy their wares; as strangers and outsiders they were considered dangerous figures. See Peggy Martin, "Drop Dead: Witchcraft Images and Ambiguities in Newfoundland Society," *Culture and Tradition*, 2 (1977), 39-41, 48-49.

[10]For a discussion of the early religious history of the island see M.F. Howley, *Ecclesiastical History of Newfoundland* (Boston: Doyle and Whittle, 1888), pp. 170-224; the grandmother of an informant on the Southern Shore received a copy of *The New Redemptorist's Book* at one of these early missions.

[11]This was a common practice at all Redemptorist missions; see *The Eikon*, 2:8 (1930), 335.

[12]Yvonne Lange, "The Household Wooden Saints of Puerto Rico" (unpublished Ph.D. dissertation, Univ. of Pennsylvania, 1975), pp. 320-27.

[13]For example see *The Eikon*, 1:6 (1929), 98.

[14]Lange, "Household Saints," pp. 197-204.

[15]Sister Mary Stephanie, "The Sacred Heart in Our Lives," *Immaculata Review*, 125-46 (June, 1979), 3; for other devotional statements see, A Priest, *The Book of the Sacred Heart of Jesus* (London: Burns, Oates and Washburne, 1935); Abbe Felix Anizan, *What Is the Sacred Heart?* Trans. Rev. John Fitzpatrick (Dublin: M.H. Gill, 1914); Louis Verheylezoon, *Devotion to the Sacred Heart: Object, Ends, Practice, Motives* (London: Sands, 1955). For a historical study of the development of this devotion see Rev. Jean V. Bainvel, *Devotion to the Sacred Heart: The Doctrine and Its History*, Trans. E. Leahy (New York: Benziger Bros. 1924).

[16]Raymond Firth, *Symbols, Public and Private* (Ithaca: Cornell Univ. Press, 1973), p. 233.

[17]For comments about these mysteries see, "The Slaves of the Immaculate Heart of Mary", in *Hail Mary Full of Grace* (Still River, Mass.: Saint Benedict Center, 1958), pp. 19-81.

[18]For a reproduction of an eighteenth century woodcut showing Our Lady of Mount Carmel see Yvonne Lange, "Lithography, an Agency of Technological Change in Religious Folk Art: A Thesis," *Western Folklore*, 33 (1974), plate opposite p. 60, figure 1; for a discussion of the connection between Mary and the wearing of the scapular see, Marina Warner, *Alone of All Her Sex: The Myth and the Cult of the Virgin Mary* (New York: Knopf, 1976), pp. 328-29; also see Mrs. Thomas Concannon, *The Queen of Ireland: An Historical Account of Ireland's Devotion to the Blessed Virgin* (Dublin: M.H. Gill, 1938), pp. 90-92. For a general discussion of the role of purgatory in popular Roman Catholicism see Gabriel Liompart, "Aspectos populares del purgatorio medieval," *Revista de Dialectologica y Tradiciones populares*, 26 (1970), 253-74.

[19]For a discussion of the iconography of St. Joseph see P.H. Ditchfield, *Symbolism of the Saints* (London and Oxford: A.R. Mowbray, 1910), pp. 16-18; George Ferguson, *Signs and Symbols in Christian Art* (London: Oxford Univ. Press, 1954), pp. 56-57; E.A. Greene, *Saints and Their Symbols* (London: Whittaker, 1911), pp. 116-17.

[20]For a background to St. Cecilia and the symbols associated with her see LeRoy H. Appleton and Stephen Bridges, *Symbolism in Liturgical Art* (New York: Scribner's Sons, 1959), p. 70; Mrs. Jameson, *Sacred and Legendary Art* (London: Longmans, Green, 1911), II, pp. 583-600; Clara Erskine Clement, *A Handbook of Christian Symbols and Stories of the Saints as Illustrated in Art*, ed. Katherine E. Conway (1886; rpt. Detroit: Gale Research, 1971), pp. 77-78.

[21]For a general discussion of the entire contents of the house as one artifact system see Gerald L. Pocius, "Calvert: A Study of Artifacts and Spatial Usage in a Newfoundland Community" (unpublished Ph.D. dissertation, Univ. of Pennsylvania, 1979), chapter 6; for a study of a specific artifact in this context see Gerald L. Pocius, "Hooked Rugs in

Newfoundland: The Representation of Social Structure in Design," *Journal of American Folklore*, 92 (1979), 273-84.

[22]For a notion of saint as mediator between the sacred and the profane see John M. Mecklin, *The Passing of the Saint: A Study of a Cultural Type* (Chicago: Univ. of Chicago Press, 1941); for a succinct statement see John M. Mecklin, "The Passing of the Saint," *American Journal of Sociology*, 24 (1919), 353-72.

[23]This theme is common in other cultures; for example, see Miles Richardson, "The Images of Christ in Spanish America as a Model for Suffering," *Journal of Inter-American Studies and World Affairs*, 13 (1971), 246-57; also see Philippe Aries, *Western Attitudes Toward Death: From the Middle Ages to the Present*, Trans. Patricia M. Ranum (Baltimore and London: Johns Hopkins Univ. Press, 1974), p. 28.

[24]G.M. Murphy, "The Mystery of Suffering," *The Eikon*, 1:6 (1929), 97.

[25]John Szwed, *Private Cultures and Public Imagery: Interpersonal Relations in a Newfoundland Peasant Society*, Newfoundland Social and Economic Studies No. 2 (St. John's: Institute of Social and Economic Research, Memorial University of Newfoundland, 1966), p. 19.

[26]Clare Cooper, "The House as Symbol of the Self," in Jon Lang, Charles Burnette and Walter Moleski, eds., *Designing for Human Behavior: Architecture and the Behavioral Sciences* (Stroudsburg, Penna.: Dowden, Hutchinson and Ross, 1974), p. 135; also see Edward O. Laumann and James S. House, "Living Room Styles and Social Attributes: The Patterning of Material Artifacts in a Modern Urban Community," *Sociology and Social Research*, 54 (1969-70), 323.

[27]For examples see Pierre Defontaines, "The Place of Believing," *Landscape*, 2:3, iii (1952-53), 26-27; J. Douglas Porteous, "Home: The Territorial Core," *Geographical Review*, 66 (1976), 390; Marion Wenzel, *House Decoration in Nubia*, Art and Society Series (Toronto: Univ. of Toronto Press, 1972), p. 39.

[28]Family altars are common in other cultures; for example see Oscar Lewis, "The Possessions of the Poor," in his *Anthropological Essays* (New York: Random House, 1970), p. 450.

[29]James W. Fernandez, "Persuasions and Performances: Of the Beast in Every Body .... And the Metaphors of Everyman," in Clifford Geertz, ed., *Myth, Symbol, and Culture* (New York: Norton, 1971), p. 58; for recent discussions of the role of metaphor in culture see James Fernandez, "The Mission of Metaphor in Expressive Culture," *Current Anthropology*, 15 (1974), 119-45; Brenda E.F. Beck, "The Metaphor as a Mediator Between Semantic and Analogic Modes of Thought," *Current Anthropology*, 19 (1978), 83-97.

Big Fish, Small Pond:
Country Musicians and Their Markets*

Neil V. Rosenberg

IN THE EARLY DECADES of this century folksong scholars sought evidence for theories about the ways in which folksongs originated and evolved by recording the songs of isolated rural peoples. Remote villages in Atlantic Canada and Appalachia were visited by scholars like Helen Creighton and Cecil Sharp. Others sought the songs of isolated occupational groups—lumbermen, cowboys and sailors. They documented a broad range of North American folksong traditions. Among these often diverse musical traditions there seemed to be a unifying characteristic: whether the singers were fishermen, farmers, cowboys or housewives, singing was for them entertainment and recreation. It was play, not work. There were some important exceptions—chanties which helped to coordinate work rhythms in the days of sail; old ballads sung by women at their housework. But even these examples showed that folksong used in work situations were adjuncts—play which made the work go more smoothly.[1]

That folksinging might be an occupation in itself, a kind of work, was not considered seriously by the people who collected folksongs in the early twentieth century in North America and Britain. The earliest ballad scholars in Britain had speculated about the possibility that folksongs were the product of minstrels or minstrel-like performers, but they were speculating about medieval rather than contemporary traditions. Although scholars recognized that professional songmakers contributed extensively to the repertoire of folksingers, they considered such songs inferior and only of interest when they had undergone some kind of evolutionary change in tune or text which transformed them into folksongs.

Recent research has revealed connections between songmaking and professional or semi-professional singers in Anglo-American folksong traditions. For example, at the turn of the century New Brunswick lumberwoods poet Joe Scott travelled the lumbercamps of Maine singing his own compositions and selling printed copies of them for ten cents a sheet. Edward D. Ives' study of Scott focuses upon his songmaking as a folk craft, but there can be no doubt that the widespread currency of Scott's compositions in the folksong traditions of eastern Canada and the northeastern U.S. reflects his self-promotion.[2] Other research has documented the careers of self-promoting folksingers in the American South during the early decades of this century, such as Richard Burnett and Blind Alfred Reed. Both were travelling professionals who marketed their own compositions as well as older traditional songs in various ways: public performance, the sale of song sheets and books, and, at the end of their careers, the selling of their own performances on phonograph records.[3]

I cite recent case studies of the early twentieth century performers because contemporary research about such individuals often overlooked their self-promotional or professional activities. Jean Thomas made J.D. Day, a blind singer and fiddler from Kentucky who recorded commercially in the twenties, into "Jilson Setters, the singing minstrel of Lost Hope Hollow," romantically obscuring the fact that he was not only a folksinger but also a modern professional who took advantage of the latest media to market his performances.[4]

Generally it is only in retrospect that folksong scholars have come to realize that some of their informants were professionals. In the twenties and thirties, American record companies and folksong collectors were sometimes recording the same individuals and groups. Usually neither knew of the other. Frequently the performers were asked for different kinds of song by each. Folksong collectors wanted the older traditional material which they recognized as folksongs, while the record company executives, after the first few years of experimentation, wanted what they considered "fresh" material. Occasionally a performer's traditional repertoire might be obscure enough to seem "fresh" to the record company, and it was the presence of recognizable folksongs on hillbilly records—like B.F. Shelton's "Pretty Polly"—which kindled the interest of folksong scholars in country music.[5] Later, folksong scholars realized that they had recorded new compositions, especially those of Jimmie Rodgers, under the impression that these "fresh" songs were old folksongs.[6]

There is now a growing body of literature on country music. It includes studies of influential performers, histories of various aspects of the music, and a range of popular and serious journals. Reissues of significant recordings have been produced (for educational purposes as well as sales to record collectors) in the U.S., Canada, Japan, Britain and Germany. That country music is related to folk music is one of the basic assumptions of this literature.

The assumption has been reinforced by studies which demonstrate aspects of the relationship. Influential performers like Bob Wills and Bill Monroe have been shown to have emerged from families and communities with strong folk music traditions.[7] Case studies of folksongs on record, such as Archie Green's work on coal mining song, have revealed much about the ways in which professional country musicians utilize folk expression.[8] One need only turn to Laws' standard index, *Native American Balladry*, for examples of hillbilly compositions now widespread in Anglo-American folksong traditions—songs like Bob Miller's "Twenty-One Years."[9]

Biographies and song histories show some ways in which folk and country music are related, but do not tell the whole story. Students of country music have traced the historical process by which radio stations and record companies—the new media—stumbled upon and came to use the vernacular music of the American South in order to make capital (just as the scholars used it for intellectual capital). Charles Wolfe, for example, has chronicled the growth of WSM's Grand Ole Opry, the influential radio show that led to Nashville's modern hegemony in country music. He stressed that most of the early Opry regulars were neither full-time professionals nor "naive hill folk preserving an exclusive and rare heritage."[10] Like Wolfe, the Cohens analyzed folk-hillbilly relationships during the early years of sound media involvement. They found that the phonograph record companies most frequently chose or were approached by people who had some experience in public or "assembly" performance traditions, terminology which I will return to later.[11]

Not all these performers had been professional folk musicians, because prior to the use of records and radio few could make a full-time living with such music. The markets of professional musicians before sound media were limited. Live performances and the sale of song texts at them reached only a small number of people. These customers could not afford to pay them enough to allow for an attractive standard of living. It is no coincidence that Richard Burnett, J.W. Day and Blind Alfred Reed were blind; had they been sighted, they would have worked in the mines, where there was more money to be earned than in singing on the courthouse square and at the county fair. The new media changed this by expanding markets, attracting advertising money and creating increased opportunity for professionalization.

Histories of early hillbilly music are illuminating insofar as they tell us about the processes from which modern country music emerged. But they do not fully explain the continuing relationship of country and folk music. The mythology which places Nashville at the center of country music, assigning certain musicians central positions in the evolutionary scheme, is just that—a mythology. There is strong evidence that the earliest recordings and radio broadcasts were in the American South.[12] There is also evidence that this media attention in part reflected stereotyped thinking about folk music by Yankee and southern urban businessmen.[13] Simon Bronner has shown that they eventually looked for such music elsewhere, in upstate New York.[14]

In fact we can take Bronner's point a step further and view country music as an example of a process which occurs when the music of a group—usually having regional, class and/or ethnic identities—achieves access to commercial media. Often this process occurs as a by-product of acculturation following migration: blues music is associated with Afro-American migration from the rural South to the urban North and West; bluegrass with Appalachian migration along a similar path; western swing with the great exodus from the Dust Bowl to California in the late thirties and early forties; and the mixture of Newfoundland, Irish and country music typified by Harry Hibbs and Dick Nolan with the great post-Confederation movement of Newfoundlanders to Toronto. Perhaps the best example of all is the continuing succession of musical styles which has accompanied a century and a half of migration from Ireland to North America. These music links tie the migrants with the homeland; they are like a cultural letter from home.[15] Indeed many of their song texts deal with such matters—comparisons of urban with rural, of new home and old. The music is the response of the migrants; the host community responds with jokes about Rastus and Liza (a libidinous black couple), hillbillies, Okies, Newfies, Pat and Mike. Often the music is stigmatized with such labels. The joking stereotypes associated with those musics deter many scholars from taking them seriously.

When it is taken seriously, often the assumption is made that as a music becomes professionalized and commercialized, its relationship with non-professional folk musics (the down/back home music) ceases. That is, historically it begins with folk and ends as pop. Since the end of World War II, country music has become a commercialized and professionalized industry in North America. Yet there is continuing evidence that it retains a relationship to folksong and folk music.

I have sought to develop a model which explains the ways in which such professionalized music, in this case country music, and folk expression are intertwined, without assuming an evolutionary historical process for the form as a whole. Instead, I believe, the very nature of a professionalized music which draws its workers from an identifiable group will inevitably affect and reflect the music traditions of the group. In other words, the music continues to function as folk music. In essence, it speaks for the group, articulating the concerns, beliefs, attitudes and world view of the group. Both content analysis and audience interviews support this point: it is not the song, its text (or the performer) which is inherently traditional, but the role of that item, the behaviors surrounding it, its function, its use and import.[16]

In 1965 D.K. Wilgus stated that a good contemporary folk musician "... may likely end up in the profession, bringing with him both the strongest influence of the professional past and new life from the nonprofessional milieu." Wilgus stressed the continuity of professional minstrelsy, pointing out that "the radio and recording industries did not invent hillbilly music." He urged folklorists to study professional hillbilly musicians.[17]

In 1965 I began interviewing professional country musicians about their personal history.[18] As Wilgus predicted, my informants' backgrounds included musical influences from both the folk and non-folk milieux. However, I found the significance of such backgrounds difficult to assess, because they often appear to have little to do with the performer's career as he views it. For example, many of the musicians I interviewed seemed to evaluate their performances in terms of income generated rather than an esthetic. Because I approached many of these interviews from the point of view of the discographer, I probably elicited responses which concentrated on the more commercial aspects of the musicians' careers.[19] However, even when I sought ethnographic and folkloristic data, my informants structured their discussions in career-oriented terms. This was especially true of younger informants whose careers were still unfolding.

The interview is a familiar type of performance for most country musicians. They regularly visit and chat "informally" with disc jockeys, fan magazine writers and other persons who "promote" or "merchandise" country music. Because he is, in econonic terms, both entrepreneur *and* product, the professional country musician uses every occasion to promote himself as "product." His role, like that of the urban bluesman, is a highly specialized and full-time one.[20] In this sense he can hardly avoid speaking of himself in career-oriented terms.

Although every professional musician's career is unique, most of the performers I have interviewed have used terminology which reflects an ideal of career "progress" and upward evolution. Such words as "amateur," "apprentice" and "professional" are used frequently. Gant's study of Nashville musicians[21] describes these terms, and I suspect that the vaguely evolutionary sequence which they imply is part of the "mazeway" or "cognitive map" of most country musicians.[22]

However, I do not intend to suggest that all country musicians see their life this way, merely that such terminology suggests ways of understanding the complex relationships between folk and popular culture in the realm of music. My model borrows from interview terminology to describe four "stages" of country music career status: apprentice, journeyman, craftsman and celebrity.[23] Although each of these categories has identifiable characteristics, I must emphasize that we are dealing with four points on a continuum, and an ideal four points at that.

What is the relation of this system to the kinds of musical performance which we call folk music? One of the problems with this model is that it encompasses a spectrum reaching from folk to mass culture; yet this is as it should be, if we are to understand the kind of process to which Wilgus alludes. However the folk end of the spectrum has been clarified by the distinctions recently set forth in independent but overlapping studies by Edward D. Ives and Anne and Norm Cohen. They suggest that there are two kinds of folk performance tradition, the domestic (or private) and the public.[24] In this study, we will be dealing with the public tradition.

It is tempting to tie the private-public distinction to the amateur-professional dichotomy of which many country musicians speak when describing their career. But the teminology of this dichotomy is so loaded with value judgments that it must be approached with great care. The word "amateur" has at least two meanings. The Latin roots of the word *denote* a person who does something for the love of it. In this literal sense the word implies nothing about skills. But in our increasingly specialized and professionalized society, "amateur" has taken on certain *connotations*.

Sometimes it is used by professional musicians to indicate a lack of skill, implying that if a musician does not make a living from music, it is because that person is musically incompetent. The word is also used to refer to a musical beginner. Here the implication is that as soon as he has the requisite skills, the amateur will become a professional.

Professionals often lump all the non-professionals under the term amateur. In reality there are many kinds of non-professional musicians in our society, from the fellow whom I overheard playing half of "Wildwood Flower" on a cheap, battered guitar at a beach in Kings County, Prince Edward Island several summers back to skilled local folk musicians like Mac Brogan of Chipman, New Brunswick, who has won fiddle contests throughout the Maritimes but, aside from the contests, plays only for his own pleasure.[25]

Moreover, professionals must rationalize to themselves and others the skilled "amateur" musicians they encounter. They point out that these people are not professionals, even though they may be good musicians, because they are not "entertainers." We will see later that there is some truth to such a statement, because non-musical skills are relevant to the kinds of audience with which the musician deals. Hence the rationalization that "amateurs" are not "entertainers" reflects a feeling of being threatened by amateurs.

Because the amateur-professional distinction is a function of the market level or scope on which each musician is operating, we will postpone further discussion of this point. At present we will concentrate upon the various levels of the musician's career status, using the four stages mentioned earlier, as shown on the chart.

Status Stage 1: Apprentice

People who consciously decide to become musicians usually do so at a relatively early age. The desire to learn leads the would-be musician to become an "apprentice." The apprentice musician learns, formally and informally, to imitate the style of one or several "models"—professional musicians—while imitating the repertoire of these models. The apprentice does his music-making either alone ("practice" or "woodshedding"), in the company of other musicians (at jam sessions, rehearsals and so forth) or in performance situations in which the roles of musician and audience are clearly and consciously defined. The apprentice musician often spends his performing time in the company of another more established musician— as a band member or "sideman" in jazz parlance—but also may be known as a performer who uses the style and songs of his model or models. Apprentice musicians tend to be preoccupied with instrumental musical skills, involved in technique for technique's sake.

Status Stage 2: Journeyman

Eventually the apprentice reaches a point at which he begins to develop his own style and accumulate his own repertoire.[26] Sometimes this occurs naturally or spontaneously; in other situations it is done consciously. At this point the musician has become a full-fledged professional, a journeyman. He has learned through his apprenticeship how to manipulate style and repertoire in order to best entertain an audience. He is no longer known as a musician who sounds like some other more well-known musician, but as a particular individual with an identifiable "sound" and repertoire.

Non-musical aspects of the musician's career become increasingly significant to the journeyman. He must learn the skills of managing the social and economic intricacies of his career in order to promote identity or "image." He becomes involved in the careers of apprentice musicians, as teacher, bandleader,[27] producer, promoter or a combination of these. His musical skill becomes important only as a means to an end—the journeyman is accepted by his audience and peers as a professional entertainer.

It is very important for the journeyman to have his "own" repertoire,

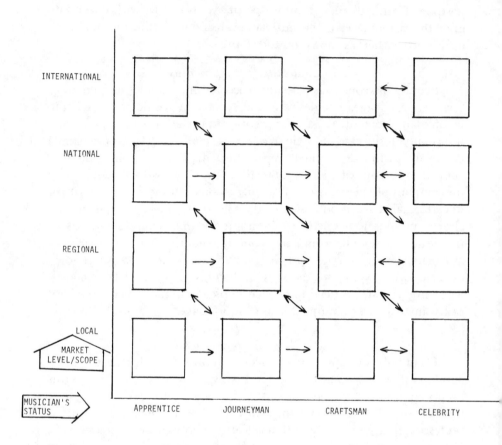

for this makes it easier for him to establish his style and thereby attract and entertain an audience. Hence, musicians in this stage are likely to become songwriters.

Status Stage 3: Craftsman

Eventually the successful journeyman becomes so well-known to his audiences that the uniqueness of his repertoire becomes relatively unimportant. At this point he has reached the "craftsman" stage. The craftsman depends upon personality, as expressed through total on-stage image or style, to attract and entertain the audience; his repertoire may include eclectic as well as unique elements, for his audience accepts him in personal terms. His basic skills at this level involve the projection of personal charisma, the facility to handle relationships with "fans" on and off-stage, and the manipulation of performance situations (emceeing the show, etc.). Both fans and promoters think of him as a "star," although that term is used rather loosely.

Status Stage 4: Celebrity

The celebrity is someone who is well-known for being well-known. There are many similarities between the celebrity and the mythic figure or the folk hero. One difference is that the celebrity rarely retains this status over a long period of time. In terms of the skills of the performer, this status level is essentially a by-product of a successful career as a craftsman. It may come about through the achievement of high income, or through repeated appearances in various media, or through noteworthy deviant behavior leading to repeated mention in various media. Rarely does it have any direct connection with the musical skills of the celebrity; for example, everyone in Newfoundland knows who Harry Hibbs is, even without having heard his records, or, if they have, without liking him. Being well known is not synonymous with being liked. For this reason the status level of celebrity is a reversible one which may or may not be of use in the performer's career.

A Word about Specialization

Thus far the discussion has dealt with the kinds of performers who are most likely to become "stars"—male vocalists. But this is only one possible specialty for a career in country music. The same steps are followed by instrumentalists, comedians, "girl singers" and others.

In each case the specialty shapes the features which delineate various status levels. For example, instrumental musicians who move from apprentice to journeyman are characterized by an identifiable "sound" and a distinctive instrumental style or technique which functions as a personal repertoire. They are valued as recording session men and band members because they know how to use their skills creatively on demand and are *not* preoccupied with technique for technique's sake.

Markets

A successful career as a professional musician involves many factors. One of the most important is a good steady income. To achieve this a professional musician must sell performances to as many people as possible, for as much money as possible, over as long a period of time as possible. I call this combination of people, money and time the *market*. It can also be conceived of as a constituency. The vertical axis of the accompanying chart has been divided into four market levels: local, regional, national and international.

As with the other axis of the chart, these levels represent points on a continuum. However, in this continuum each level subsumes the one below it. A regional market consists of a group of local markets, a national market includes a group of regions, and so forth. A single consumer may in some instances be part of the international market (when she buys a Charlie Pride record) and in others be part of the local market (when she hears a local musician performing at the neighborhood tavern). But the musician must work his way up, starting on the lowest market level. Each market has special characteristics.

Local Markets

Musicians working within the local market, a city or county, do not go on the road. It is possible for them to hold a "day job," and because local markets offer limited economic return, it may be necessary to have such a job. The local market musician does most of his performing before live audiences, and receives relatively little pay. Local markets offer little opportunity for mass media exposure. Television and radio appearances are limited usually to local talent shows or other "special appearance" situations. The musician who wishes to sell his performances on phonograph records must do so at his own expense.

Regional Markets

A region may range from a group of cities or counties through a province or state to an aggregation of provinces or states. In these markets, live audiences are larger and must pay more to hear the performer. In addition, the regional performer has some regular access to radio and television, and is likely to have his performances marketed by a regionally-based record company. The performer must tour the region extensively, appearing in bars, at fairs and similar events, and occasionally in concerts.

People pay more to see the regional-market professional, and his income is potentially greater than that of the local market performer.

National and International Markets

At this level, the professional's recordings are sold by major record companies; his appearances on television and radio are on large stations or network outlets or syndications; and he plays before live audiences mainly on concert tours in large cities. If he plays in bars, they are places where the drinks are expensive and cover charges are levied. International markets represent a continuation of the same phenomenon on a wide scale of distribution and income.

From this brief description of market levels, it can be understood why greater exposure in the mass media is generally equated with higher income. Professional country musicians tend to seek ways to reach larger markets. These ways generally involve altering style and repertoire in order to fit a new context and create a new "image."[28] For example, the country singer may add or have added to his recordings a string section, in the hope that this will appeal to more record buyers and will expand his market from regional to national. Because he thinks of himself as not just a musician but an entertainer, he is willing to alter style and repertoire in order to "sell" his "image" to a larger potential audience.[29] The larger the market, the more pressure there is for him to change, to "keep up with the times."[30] This is because he is competing with many other professionals for a national market consisting of local and regional groups having widely varying tastes.

The higher up the market scale the performer rises, the more impersonal and uncertain performer-audience relationships become. Decisions about repertoire, style, performance context and other aspects of career are determined less by direct feedback from the audience. Mass culture mechanisms—trade charts, sales figures, the opinions of others inside the music business—become increasingly important and usually add to the pressure for change.

But the country musician must act with some restraint in the alteration of style and repertoire while seeking new markets. He cannot afford to lose his basic local or regional markets—those who will go regularly to see him perform "in person," buy all his records and join his fan club. An abrupt change may alienate this audience, even if it sells his records to some people who have not heard him before.[31] Few professionals can make their living solely from record sales. The musician is aware of this and knows that within any market some people are more important than others, because they will pay more consistently to hear him. The musician's market is like the politician's constituency. Like the politician, the musician has principles and is only willing to compromise to a certain point.

As the chart shows, a musician who wishes to improve his professional standing by moving to a broader market must not only alter his style and repertoire while attempting to keep his old audiences pleased; he must also accept a drop in status. When a musician who has established himself as a journeyman in the local market enters the regional marketplace, it is as an apprentice. Conversely, a move to a small market means a rise in status. A journeyman in the national marketplace may "retire" to a secure niche as a local celebrity. Hence the title of this paper.

There exists within country music a hierarchy of musicians stretching from face-to-face situations which would clearly fit all the defining criteria for folksong, to mass media situations which we generally describe as popular culture. Some country musicians are recognized craftsmen or journeymen in a small local market; they are also apprentices to the journeymen and craftsmen whose community or audience is regional or national. Professional country musicians constantly face decisions pertaining to their position within this hierarchy. The move from a smaller to a larger market is a gamble. There is potentially more income and greater fame to be gained; there is also more chance for failure, rejection and insecurity.

The seeking of a larger market is part of the general strategy of income maximization which any self-employed professional follows. Often differences of opinion arise between the performer and those who market his performances. The performer generally perceives his career in terms of a long span of time, as something which he can build; whereas the bookers and record companies who share in the profits from his performances are anxious to make as much money in a short period of time as possible. Given this recurrent conflict, professionals often seek ways of spreading their risk by investing in businesses (often connected with music—music stores, publishing companies), by managing and promoting other artists, and by developing other roles within the industry (disc jockey, recording company representative, etc.).

When we realize that the local folk performer, a celebrated craftsman within the community, is potentially or in actuality an anonymous apprentice within a national situation, then questions of change and continuity within local musical traditions become more understandable. Feedback from popular to folk music follows the hierarchy.[32] Those with wider markets serve as teachers and models to those whose market is more localized.[33] On each level the journeyman or craftsman uses the styles and repertoires of his models as a base for personalized performances which attract and entertain his market. He does this by selecting those elements of performance style and repertoire content most nearly matching those which he knows the market likes. Thus he is both a mirror and an instrument of folk and popular tastes.[34] Every local folk style and repertoire reflects a combination of regionally popular models; regionally popular styles and repertoire reflect nationally popular models, and so forth.

I do not wish to give the impression that I am merely updating the concept of "gesunkenes kulturgut" by describing a one-way process. Local style and repertoire are constantly being introduced to regional and national markets by professionals who draw upon their "background" for unique elements which they can "sell" and thereby move up within the hierarchy which I have just described.[35] In this way there is also feedback from folk to popular music, and this is precisely what Wilgus means when he alludes to "new life from the non-professional milieu."[36]

The movement of performers through various market levels and status stages may involve the use of folk traditions in various ways. Several examples can be found in the career of Dick Nolan, a native of Corner Brook, Newfoundland.[37] In 1964 he was leading the "house band" at Toronto's Horseshoe Club, the well-known country music nightclub in Ontario. He was a journeyman in a regional market. Many of his regular audience were, like him, transplanted Newfoundlanders. As he told one interviewer: " ... wherever you go, if you go to Toronto or you go to the States and if you're looking for Newfoundlanders, you just got to look for country music and you'll find them."[38] Because Toronto is an economic and a population center, Nolan's status enabled him to obtain a recording contract in 1963 with a small "independent" record company, Arc Records. His recordings for Arc, ostensibly aimed at a national market but in fact marketed primarily in those areas of eastern Canada in which there were Newfoundlanders, were of the kind we might expect with an apprentice: "covers" of other performers' hits and collections of familiar (mainly traditional) songs from Newfoundland. His first record did not even carry his name: the songs (Johnny Cash hits) were expected to attract purchasers, not the singer. Over a five year period he gradually became established as a singer of Johnny Cash material and Newfoundland songs; Arc began distributing his records on a national basis. At this point he was able to negotiate a contract with a "major" record company, RCA. Here he began to record his own unique material, marking his emergence as a journeyman on the national level.

This is an example of an upward move in market accompanied by a step back in status; Nolan had to establish himself as a successful national apprentice on records before he was able to move into the journeyman status. Music from his own region's traditions played a part in this process;

four albums of Newfoundland and Atlantic Canadian songs helped him pass his apprenticeship. It should be noted that these songs were familiar to most record buyers from the region; the albums were aimed at people who would purchase recordings of the songs even if they did not know the singer. Although distributed nationally, they were clearly aimed at two regional markets: the Newfoundland market, where Nolan returned periodically for "tours," and the Toronto market, consisting of Newfoundlanders and Maritimers who frequented the clubs where he appeared.

When Nolan made his move to RCA, he very quickly had his first national "hit," with a song which he co-wrote with Ellis Coles—"Aunt Martha's Sheep." This functioned as the "original" material expected of a journeyman, but was in fact a little-known local folksong from Newfoundland which Nolan "collected" from Coles. More importantly, it was a hit because it also functioned as a folksong—telling a story of real immediacy to Newfoundlanders.

Set in a Newfoundland community, it narrates the adventures of the young men who steal Aunt Martha's sheep. It is butchered and cooked, and they are having a "feed" when the Mountie who, like all Mounties, is not a native of the province in which he is posted, arrives at the door. They invite him in, telling him they are having moose, and offer him a meal. He accepts and as the song ends, it is the Mountie who "ate the most." Michael Taft's study of this song points out that the outsmarting of a mainland official in Nolan's version of the song replaces the scene in earlier versions in which the gullible official was a representative from the local police force, the Newfoundland Rangers (disbanded when Newfoundland became part of Canada).[39] Nolan's song, in which Newfies outwit a mainlander, became popular at a time when Newfie jokes, most of which portray Newfoundlanders as fools, were popular in the rest of Canada. No doubt this accounts in part for the great popularity of the song.

Thus Nolan utilized folk traditions in two very different ways in order to advance his career: first in recording familiar material, second in recording "unique" material. His success with "Aunt Martha's Sheep" came shortly after his return to Newfoundland. This was a downward move in market and as might be expected, entailed a forward step in status. In St. John's he was recognized as a craftsman, and soon had his own weekly television show. During the following years he recorded a number of other "original" songs (including a sequel to "Aunt Martha's Sheep"), some traditional, others newly composed, and became a regional celebrity.

Since then, his career has not had the same spectacular progress as it had in the early seventies. Typically, his celebrity status was temporary, and as a craftsman in the Newfoundland regional market he found that his career development was limited by the size of the population and amount of available cash. In the late seventies he sold his home in Newfoundland and returned to Ontario, a larger and more lucrative regional market. In this move he was not going from one status to another, nor was he changing his market scope; he was just moving from one regional market to another. Hence this move was not accompanied or accomplished by any kind of change in style or image as were the earlier moves.

The sum total of this activity by Nolan during the period 1963-78 was the recyling of both familiar and obscure Newfoundland folksongs from earlier oral, print and recorded sources to a new generation of Newfoundlanders in two provinces via sound media and in-person performances. Many of the songs which Nolan recorded following his success with "Aunt Martha's Sheep" dealt in some way with identifiably Newfoundland topics, and Nolan's success encouraged other songwriters to create country songs about Newfoundland topics, or at least to record them, for Nolan was by no means the first Newfoundlander to write songs about local or regional topics in the format of country music.[40]

Country musicians often use traditional material as a part of their career marketing strategy. Elsewhere I described the case of New Brunswick disc jockey/songwriter "Goodtime Charlie" Russell, who utilized the Miramichi tradition of satirical poetry in a successful political lampoon which brought him national recognition within Canadian country music.[41] Neither Russell nor Nolan, nor any other professional like them, uses traditional material or techniques merely because they are traditional.[42] The Blue Sky Boys, a brother duo from Appalachian North Carolina, chose the songs in their repertoire because of the world view presented in the song lyrics, not because of the song's age or traditional pedigree. That they did record and perform a substantial number of older folksongs reflected the fact that such songs were, in their estimation, commercially viable and that the lyrics of these songs conveyed a message which they approved.[43]

In this paper I have shown that in the realm of country music, performers manipulate their repertoire to advance their career while at the same time presenting songs which are ideologically and stylistically acceptable to their audiences. The interests of performer and audience must overlap if the interaction between the two is to be successful; in this sense what I have presented is merely an elaboration of the ideas about the personal and rhetorical use of folklore performance as advanced by Abrahams, Bauman and others. What makes my argument somewhat different from theirs is that I draw no clear-cut dividing line between small-group and mass audience performance. Instead I describe a broad spectrum. The interpretation of audience or market size as a defining characteristic of folklore presents a dilemma which folklore scholars create in using a performance-based definition of their subject, if it is indeed a dilemma and not a widening of perspective. I leave that question for future studies.

Notes

*Earlier versions of this paper were presented at the 1972 meeting of the American Folklore Society and the 1978 meeting of the Folklore Studies Association of Canada. Thanks to Patricia Averill, Lisa Feldman, Scott Hambly, Martin Laba, Peter Narváez, Richard A. Peterson, Mayne Smith, Herb Trotman and Wilfred Wareham for reading and commenting on various drafts. Portions of the research reported here were made possible through a Canada Council Leave Fellowship (W74-0346).

[1]For a further discussion of this point, see Roger D. Abrahams, "Toward a Sociological Theory of Folklore: Performing Services," *Western Folklore*, 37 (1978), 162.

[2]Edward D. Ives, *Joe Scott: The Woodsman-Songmaker* (Urbana: Univ. of Illinois Press, 1978).

[3]Charles K. Wolfe, "Man of Constant Sorrow: Richard Burnett's Story," *Old Time Music*, 9 (Summer 1973), 6-9 and 10 (Autumn 1973), 5-11; and Rounder Collective (Ken Irwin, Bruce Kaplan, Marian Leighton, Bill Nowlin), brochure (8 pages) to Rounder 1001, *How Can A Poor Man Stand Such Times And Live?* . . . The Songs of Blind Alfred Reed (12" 33 1/3 rpm disc, 1972).

[4]See D.K. Wilgus, *Anglo-American Folksong Scholarship Since 1898* (New Brunswick, N.J.: Rutgers Univ. Press, 1959), p. 205.

[5]B.F. Shelton, "Pretty Polly," Victor 35838 (10" 78 rpm disc, ca. 1928). That this was a version of an old English broadside ballad was noted by Herbert Halpert in "Some Recorded American Folk Song," *The American Music Lover*, II (Nov. 1936), 197. It was reissued on County 522, *Old-Time Ballads from the Southern Mountains* (12" 33 1/3 rpm disc, 1969).

[6]John Greenway, "Jimmie Rodgers—A Folksong Catalyst," *Journal of American Folklore*, 70 (1957), 231-234.

[7]For Wills, see Charles R. Townsend, *San Antonio Rose* (Urbana: Univ. of Illinois Press, 1976); for Monroe, see Ralph Rinzler, "Bill Monroe," in *Stars of Country Music*, ed. Bill C. Malone and Judith McCulloh (Urbana: Univ. of Illinois Press, 1975), pp. 202-221.

[8]Archie Green, *Only a Miner* (Urbana: Univ. of Illinois Press, 1971).

[9]G. Malcolm Laws, Jr., *Native American Balladry* (Philadelphia: American Folklore Society, 1964, rev.), p. 184. Laws does not mention Miller's authorship of this song. Other examples: "The Lawson Family" (pp. 208-209), "Floyd Collins" (pp. 223-224), "The Wreck of Number Nine" (p. 225). Many other songs in Laws' index could be shown to have been influenced by versions recorded or otherwise performed by "hillbilly" entertainers, as with "Ten Broeck and Mollie" (pp. 242-243).

[10]Charles K. Wolfe, *The Grand Ole Opry: The Early Years, 1925-35* (London: Old Time Music, 1975), p. 17.

[11]Anne and Norm Cohen, "Folk and Hillbilly Music: Further Thoughts on Their Relation," *JEMF Quarterly* 13 (1977), 50-57.

[12]Richard A. Peterson and Russell Davis, Jr., "The Fertile Crescent of Country Music," *Journal of Country Music*, 6 (1975), 19-27.

[13]Archie Green, "Hillbilly Music: Source and Symbol," *Journal of American Folklore*, 78 (1965), 204-228.

[14]Simon J. Bronner, "The Country Music Tradition in Western New York State," *Journal of Country Music*, 7:1 (actually mislabeled as 6:4; January 1978), 29-46, 55-58.

[15]See D.K. Wilgus, "Country-Western Music and the Urban Hillbilly," *Journal of American Folklore*, 83 (1970), 154-184.

16This perspective is suggested by Bronner, "Western New York," 46, 55-58; and reflects the approach of Charles Keil in *Urban Blues* (Chicago: Univ. of Chicago Press, 1966).

17D.K. Wilgus, "An Introduction to the Study of Hillbilly Music," *Journal of American Folklore*, 78 (1965), 203, 197.

18See, for example, my articles "The Osborne Brothers, Part I," *Bluegrass Unlimited* (Sept. 1971), 5-10 and "The Osborne Brothers, Part II," *Bluegrass Unlimited* (Feb. 1972), 5-8.

19For discussion of the theories and techniques of discography, see: Ed Kahn, "Will Roy Hearne: Peripheral Folk Song Scholar," *Western Folklore*, 23 (1964), 173-179; Scott Hambly, "Mac Wiseman: A Discographic Enigma," *JEMF Quarterly*, 7 (1971), 53-58; Norman Cohen, "Computerized Hillbilly Discography: The Gennett Project," *Western Folklore*, 30 (1971), 183-193; and Archie Green, "A Discography/Biography Journey: The Martin-Roberts-Martin 'Aggregation'," *Western Folklore*, 30 (1971), 194-201. A useful study in applied discography is Robert Dixon and John Godrich, *Recording the Blues* (New York and London: Studio Vista, 1970).

20See Keil, pp. 154-155.

21Alice M. Gant, "The Musicians in Nashville," *The Journal of Country Music*, 3 (1972), 24-44.

22The terms "mazeway" and "cognitive map" have been used by anthropologist Anthony F.C. Wallace to describe the way in which individuals perceive their culture. See Wallace, *Culture and Personality* (New York: Random House, 1970) and "Revitalization Movements," *American Anthropologist*, 58 (1956), 264-281.

23A parallel use of this terminology is given by Alan P. Merriam who in discussing an African professional wandering minstrel contrasts this "craftsman" with "the journeyman chorus member," asking if there is any difference between their roles. *The Anthopology of Music* (Evanston: Northwestern Univ. Press, 1964), p. 213.

24Edward D. Ives, "Lumbercamp Singing and the Two Traditions," *Canadian Folk Music Journal*, 5 (1977) 21; Anne and Norm Cohen, 54.

25As Charles Seeger concluded, "We cannot ... class folk music, as a whole, as an amateur idiom." See his "Professionalism and Amateurism in the Study of Folk Music," in *The Critics and the Ballad*, ed. MacEdward Leach and Tristram P. Coffin (Carbondale, Ill.: Univ. of Southern Illinois Press, 1961), p. 155. As with any folklore form, it is important to distinguish between individual competence and ideals of performance.

26Well-known bluegrass musician Ralph Stanley stated, "... we found out that it didn't pay to imitate anybody else." Frank Taylor, Linda Johnson and Rich Kirby, "Ralph Stanley: '...It's Bound to Be Natural'," *Mountain Life and Work* (Dec. 1972), 7. See also Ralph Rinzler, "Ralph Stanley: The Tradition from the Mountains," *Bluegrass Unlimited*, 8:9 (March 1974), 7-11.

27Through such apprenticeship patterns, musical substyles may develop. See James Rooney, *Bossmen: Bill Monroe and Muddy Waters* (New York: Dial Press, 1972), a study of two professionals whose styles apprentice sidemen have helped to perpetuate. A good band leader is like a good coach. He knows the strengths and weaknesses of each man, and learns how to get the best performance out of each of his players.

28Repertoire change occurs in every folk tradition, even the relatively conservative Anglo-American folksong tradition. See Henry Glassie, Edward D. Ives and John Szwed, *Folk Songs and Their Makers* (Bowling Green, Ohio: Bowling Green University Popular Press, 1970). However, professional songmakers, even those "schooled" in and "loyal" to this conservative tradition, make different and more extensive changes. See John Quincy Wolf, "Folksingers and the Re-Creation of Folksong," *Western Folklore*, 26 (1967), 101-111, especially his discussion of Jimmy Driftwood and Earnest B. "Pop" Stoneman, 109-110.

29For discussions of such alterations in style and repertoire, see Scott Hambly, "Mac Wiseman," 56-57, and Frederick E. Danker, "The Repertory and Style of a Country Singer: Johnny Cash," *Journal of American Folklore*, 85 (1972), 309-329.

30See, for example, Bill Littleton, "Earl Scruggs Still Wants to Break New Ground," *Country Music* (Oct. 1972), 50-52.

[31]See Lester Flatt's comments to this point, regarding his recording of Bob Dylan songs for Columbia Records—Pete Kuykendall, "Lester Flatt and the Nashville Grass," *Bluegrass Unlimited* (Jan. 1971), 3.

[32]William Ferris, Jr. cites Harold Courlander's use of the term "feedback" to describe this process with regard to blues recordings, and notes the existence of "a similar process" with regard to hillbilly recordings—*Blues from the Delta* (London: Studio Vista, 1970), p. 91.

[33]Ferris, pp. 97-98.

[34]A good description of a local celebrity is Charles S. Guthrie's " 'Whitey' Stearns: Troubadour of the Cumberland Valley," *Kentucky Folklore Record*, 18 (1972), 52-55.

[35]See Green, *Only a Miner*, for case histories.

[36]Wilgus, "An Introduction," 203.

[37]Information about Nolan comes in part from a 1971 interview with him in St. John's, Newfoundland by I. Sheldon Posen, on deposit at the Memorial University of Newfoundland Folklore and Language Archive (MUNFLA), accession number 73-45, tapes C1399-1401. A partial listing of Nolan's recordings appears in Michael Taft, *A Regional Discography of Newfoundland and Labrador, 1904-1972* (St. John's: Memorial Univ. of Newfoundland, 1975), pp. 29-35.

[38]MUNFLA 73-45, C1399, sd. 1.

[39]Michael Taft, "Of Scoffs, Mounties, and Mainlanders: The Popularity of a Sheep-Stealing Ballad in Newfoundland," read at the 1975 meeting of the American Folklore Society. See Taft's essay in this volume.

[40]For further material on country music in Newfoundland, see: Gordon Cox, "Some Aspects of Musical Acculturation in the Repertoire of a Newfoundland Singer," *Culture & Tradition*, 2 (1977), 91-104; Peter Narváez, "Country and Western in Diffusion: Juxtaposition and Syncretism in the Popular Music of Newfoundland," *Culture & Tradition*, 2 (1977), 105-114; Peter Narváez, "The Folk Parodist," *Canadian Folk Music Journal*, 5 (1977), 32-37; Sheldon Posen and Michael Taft, "The Newfoundland Popular Music Project," *Canadian Folk Music Journal*, 1 (1973), 17-23; and Michael Taft, " 'That's Two More Dollars': Jimmy Linegar's Success with Country Music in Newfoundland," *Folklore Forum*, 7 (1974), 99-121.

[41]Neil V. Rosenberg, "Goodtime Charlie and the Bricklin: A Satirical Song in Context," *Canadian Oral History Association Journal*, 3 (1978), 27-46.

[42]There is some evidence that attempts to adhere to tradition and resist change in music lead to an over-stressing of those elements in the style which are stereotyped by outside cultures as typical, leading to a kind of mannerism. See Ruth Katz, "Mannerism and Culture Change: An Ethnomusicological Example," *Current Anthropology*, ii (1970), 465-475.

[43]David E. Whisnant, " 'Our Type of Song': A Second Look at the Blue Sky Boys," in brochure accompanying JEMF 104, *Presenting the Blue Sky Boys* (12: 33 1/3 rpm disc, 1976), 6-12.

Contributors

James Hornby holds masters degrees in literature from Concordia University and folklore from Memorial University in Newfoundland. He is the former editor of *The Island Magazine*, an award winning historical publication sponsored by the Prince Edward Island Historical Foundation.

Martin Laba is an Assistant Professor in the Department of Communication at Simon Fraser University, and a writer and broadcaster in radio and television in Vancouver, British Columbia. He has contributed articles to journals in folklore and communication studies, has recently completed production of a television documentary, "Video, Vinyl and Culture," a program on the history and development of rock video, and is currently working on a book with Richard S. Gruneau entitled, *Popular Culture and Social Process: Canadian Experiences.*

Martin Lovelace is an Assistant Professor of Folklore at Memorial University of Newfoundland. He is the author of numerous academic articles dealing with folklore and literature, folk narrative and oral biography.

Robert S. McCarl, Jr. received his Ph.D. in folklore at Memorial University of Newfoundland and is an Assistant Professor of Folklore in the Anthropology Department at the University of South Carolina. A leading scholar in occupational folklore studies, he is the author of an occupational folklife analysis of firefighters, *Good Fire/Bad Night.*

Peter Narváez is an Assistant Professor and Associate Director of the Folklore and Language Archive, Memorial University of Newfoundland. He is Chairperson of the Association for the Study of Canadian Radio and Television / Atlantic Region, and is a member of that organization's national executive board. The author of academic articles concerning a variety of folksong, folk narrative and popular culture topics, he has also produced several long playing records, and hosted and performed on his own blues shows for CBC (Canadian Broadcasting Corporation) Radio.

Gerald L. Pocius is an Associate Professor of Folklore at Memorial University of Newfoundland and the Vice President of the Society for the Study of Architecture in Canada. He is the author of many material culture studies, including *Textile Traditions in Eastern Newfoundland.*

Neil V. Rosenberg is a Professor of Folklore and the Director of the Memorial University of Newfoundland Folklore and Language Archive. A folklorist and ethnomusicologist with strong interests in history and popular culture, he has edited *Folklore and Oral History* and is the author of *Bluegrass: A History*.

Paul Smith is a researcher at the Centre for English Cultural Tradition and Language at the University of Sheffield, an academic unit which in conjunction with the Department of Folklore, Memorial University of Newfoundland, sponsors the Institute for Folklore Studies in England and Canada. His principal fields of interest are folksong, folk narrative and Canadian folklore. *The Book of Nasty Legends* is his most recent publication.

Michael Taft received his Ph.D. in folklore from Memorial University of Newfoundland in 1977. Presently he is a freelance folklorist working out of Saskatoon, Saskatchewan. Among his recent books are *Travelling the Outports: Two Studies in Newfoundland Itinerant Culture* (1981), *Tall Tales of British Columbia* (1983), and *Discovering Saskatchewan Folklore* (1983).